DREAMS

DREAMS
Soul-Centered Living
in the 21st Century

A Depth Psychological and Somatic
Approach to Achieving Transformation

Laura V. Grace, PhD

AEON

Revised edition published in 2020 by
Aeon Books
PO Box 76401
London W5 9RG

British Library Cataloguing in Publication Data

A C.I.P. for this book is available from the British Library

ISBN-13: 978-1-91280-790-1

Typeset by Medlar Publishing Solutions Pvt Ltd, India
Printed in Great Britain

www.aeonbooks.co.uk

The author gratefully acknowledges permission to quote from the following:

"Dreams" by Mary Oliver, from *Dream Work*, published by Grove Atlantic, 1986. Reprinted by permission.

"What to Remember When Waking" by David Whyte from the *House of Belonging*, published by Many Rivers Press, 1996. Reprinted by permission.

This book is dedicated to my amazing life partner and husband, Thomas, who provides the loving space to share and explore our nighttime dreams, every single day. And, to my late mother, who believed in the significance of my dreams and encouraged me to write them down and heed their wisdom.

PRAISE FOR DREAMS: SOUL-CENTERED LIVING IN THE 21ST CENTURY

Laura Grace speaks to readers in a lyrical voice, inviting us to greet the gift of our dreams with gratitude. Her willingness to share the process of working her own dreams provides a model for self-reflection and dream exploration. This approach to dream work connects us to the language of our souls in a rich and meaningful way. *Dreams: Soul-Centered Living in the 21st Century* guides us in the process of developing a relationship with our dreams that facilitates our ongoing healing.

—Jeanne Mar Schul, PhD, RSMT, Berry College &
Pacifica Graduate Institute

Have you ever wanted to know what your dreams really mean? Laura Grace's powerful new book explains clearly and simply how to understand what your own inner wisdom is trying to tell you every night.

—James Wawro, author, *Ask Your Inner Voice*

Get out your highlighters! Laura Grace's book is filled with practical yet profound information that will open a mystic gateway into the remarkable realm of your dreams. Destined to be a classic. Highly recommended!

—Denise Linn, author, *Hidden Power of Dreams*
and founder, Gateway Dreaming Institute

Illuminated with a treasury of personal anecdotes, rich examples, and colorful imagery, Laura Grace beckons us to consider the possibility of transformation through engagement with the realm we navigate every night. *Dreams: Soul-Centered Living in the 21st Century* successfully endeavors to make this strange and often obscure realm intriguingly accessible.

—Michael Stillwater, founder, theGreatSong.net, author,
Grace In Practice, and *Passports: Notes from Borderlands*

CONTENTS

ACKNOWLEDGMENTS

With great respect and appreciation, I acknowledge all the dreamers who have shared their nighttime phantasms with me. This book contains dreams from some special students and clients whose soulful messages will inspire others interested in using dreams as a potent guide for transformation. I also want to thank my editor and friend, Elyn Selu, for tending to the soul of this book with her artful eye, and for the other amazing people who have encouraged me to share my dream work with the world.

INTRODUCTION

The overall subject of our dreams is, ultimately, the inner process of individuation. Most dreams, in one way or another, are portrayals of our individual journeys toward wholeness. They show us the stages along the way—the adventures, obstacles, conflicts, and reconciliations that lead finally to a sense of the self.

—Robert Johnson

Imagine walking into a dark theater. Hundreds of empty seats await an audience to sit in before a shadowy stage. The director shouts, "Lights, cameras, action!" and you are mesmerized as the actors take their places and the storyline begins to unfold. As you watch, you feel yourself both watching the movie and being *in* the movie. The plot twists and turns as you connect with the actors and every dream character is playing a unique role. Feelings of excitement, judgment, bias, disdain, fear, hatred, empathy, love, and compassion arise. The film captivates your every sense and the images feel alive in your body. As the movie ends and the credits roll you realize that this wasn't just any movie, it is a story about *your* life.

And, so it is.

You are the screen writer, director, producer, casting agent, choreographer, landscape artist, and every character starring in your nightly dreams. You are also the observer who witnesses a comedy, tragedy, romance, horror film called "This Is My Life." All of these creative gestures and more emerge from your unconscious an average of four to five times per night. Every film, crafted by you, reveals your unresolved issues, desires, hopes, fears, strengths, doubts, grief, resentments, beliefs, and connections to the deepest realms of your soul. And it doesn't stop there; dreams are not always purely personal and can encompass the "anima mundi," the Latin term for "world soul."

Dreams are the language of our individual and collective soul. The word "soul" stems from the Greek term "psyche." Carl Jung (1963) declared: "Without the psyche there would be neither knowledge nor insight." During dreamtime, while the ego is asleep, psyche comes to life and reveals information unattainable during waking life.

As a prolific dreamer, I became interested in connecting and understanding my dreams when I was eight years old. By age sixteen, I was dreaming about events which inevitably manifested the following day. My mother kept urging, "Write down your dreams, Laura, they are trying to tell you something important," and thus began my personal and spiritual journey with dreams. Now, more than thirty years later, I have bookcases and boxes filled with dream journals. They are treasure troves of thoughts, feelings, and wisdom about my family, physical health, past relationships, finances, life's purpose, shadow aspects, fears, insecurities, self-sabotaging behaviors, desires, strengths, and spiritual gifts. Dreams are the purest form of information. Since they are not censored by our conscious thoughts, feelings, and perceptions, they possess the capacity to provide more support and insight than therapy, and they are free! I am always saddened when people tell me their dreams are nonsensical or that they do not have time to listen to them. Our dreams are wellsprings of information, the language of our soul.

You dream every night whether you remember your dreams or not. The more you seek to understand them, the more likely you will recall them. The first thing to keep in mind is that *your dreams are meant to help you, not frighten or confuse you.* I cannot tell you how many people have secretly shared that they do not listen to their dreams, or remember their dreams, because they are afraid of them, or they will have to make some significant changes. Growth can be messy and change is inevitable if you wish to grow. You always have the choice to delve inward and move forward, and you have control over when you choose to do so.

Second, all dreams are meaningful despite how ridiculous they may seem, even "snippets" contain invaluable information. Dreams may seem silly but only to the limitations of your waking mind. Even working with one dream image will help you increase your self-awareness and can lead to significant breakthroughs.

After having taught more than 200 dream courses, the technique I employ is an "embodied" process, meaning I teach people how to connect with the characters, symbols, feelings, landscape—every aspect of the dream as though it is "a living experience." Therefore, this book does not contain a dream symbol list nor does it provide quick and easy ways to interpret your dreams. Dreams create a link between your daily awareness and the unconscious realm and are highly personal to you, the dreamer. Ultimately, *you* recognize what your dreams are truly trying to convey. You do not need to spend a lot of time and effort in order to understand your dreams, but the intention to befriend your dreams and the commitment to working with them is necessary. *Dreams: Soul-Centered Living in the 21st Century* provides some of today's most insightful, spiritually and scientifically potent practical teachings for those who are ready and willing to understand the infinite power of their dreams. It covers some basic information on dreams such as dream recall, working with dream characters, and common dream themes. The material reaches into the transformational path of archetypes, alchemy, numinous dreams, Waking Dreaming™ and Somatic Dream Expression™ (two unique dream processes I created which are thoroughly covered in Chapters 8 and 9).

Each chapter uses actual nighttime dreams to illustrate how you can clearly understand your own dreams. And at the end of each chapter you are invited to "Put it into practice!" by applying practical dream practices designed to connect you with your dreams so you may move toward what Jung called "individuation." The path of individuation is the process of becoming aware of one's whole self and encompasses the personal unconscious and the collective unconscious. Both of these realms can be witnessed through the remarkable world of dreams.

As I am writing this introduction, I received a dream from a student, a dream of transformation that was painful yet liberating. The touchstone image was a fragmented portrait of Pegasus which I found interesting. Jung regarded Pegasus as a symbol of spiritual energy since

Pegasus is a magical creature in Greek mythology and is typically portrayed as a white horse with divine qualities. Pegasus is also known as "The Thundering Horse of Jove" because he brought thunder and lightning from Mt. Olympus as instructed by Zeus. Pegasus fortified a place as a constellation in the Northern Hemisphere sky in honor of his tenacious assistance to Zeus. The image of Pegasus is unforgettable: a formidable and gorgeous white horse with wings, graced with the strength and ability to fly. Every dream possesses what I call a "touchstone," an image that provides the dreamer with healing energy. In the case of my student, I encouraged him to continue working with the dream image of Pegasus as an image that is alive and is his touchstone. As he more deeply understands his dream and the wisdom it imparts around some old, unresolved trauma, the image will evolve and may transform from fragmented to whole and complete.

Since dreams are a powerful pathway to transformation, "Pegasus" is the dream image I am relying upon as I write this book. May my words inspire and touch you, the reader and dreamer, and support you on your pathway to wholeness.

Laura V. Grace

CHAPTER SECTIONS

Chapter 1 discusses the numinous nature of your dreams and how significant they are to every area of your life: relationships, health, finances, career, your soul's calling and more. We conclude this information-packed chapter by exploring the seven steps to total dream recall and how to successfully tap into their unlimited information *right now*.

Chapter 2 examines common dream themes. Although dreams are frequently personal and meant for you, the dreamer, there are a variety of subjects that commonly arise during dreamtime. We will look at a few of the most popular themes and identify what they might mean for you.

Chapter 3 helps you decode the language of your dreams. Six essential keys to self-awareness are underscored to help you understand the power of your dreams and their specific meaning that is uniquely meant for you. The four different levels of dream are also discussed: physical, issue-related/intellectual, emotional and spiritual. The soul speaks in metaphor and you will learn how to approach dreams with an open mind while employing the art of inquiry.

Chapter 4 centers on our greatest challenges and rewards when working with dreams: dream characters. Is the figure a woman, man, someone familiar, a complete stranger or someone with whom you are currently in relationship? We explore all of these possibilities and more then conclude with developing your personal dream character list.

Chapter 5 reveals the hidden power of Eros, Thanatos, anima, animus and shadow archetypes. Special attention is given to the value of learning to balance your feminine and masculine aspects and the "divine marriage" which results from integrating the anima and animus. Facing both the dark and light sides of the shadow is also covered in detail.

Chapter 6 reveals the power of the "living image" and employs Carl Jung's process of active imagination and amplification. All dream images are viewed as gifts that psyche offers us and as soon as we attempt to interpret a symbol we lose its meaning. Dream images possess intelligence, depth, and a persona of their own. Learn how to work with your dream images while practicing open-mindedness and curiosity.

Chapter 7 investigates nightmares and how they are beneficial tools for transformation. We investigate some common nightmare themes and how to safely face your fears by taking action, working with "friendly" dream figures and hitting the "pause button."

Chapter 8 delves into dreams of healing by addressing symptoms that adversely affect the body, mind, and soul. Using real life examples, addiction and physical ailments are tended to with the power of dream images.

Chapter 9 explores *Eco-dreams* and our connection with the natural world. Since we are interconnected to the web of life, eco-dreaming connect us to the doorway of our ecological self. Grief dreams are also studied and how they can help us evolve.

Chapter 10 dives into cutting edge dream work called *Somatic Dreams*. Body-based dreams are unforgettable because we actually "feel" them in our bodies. This chapter discusses how somatic dream images can lead to profound insight. We conclude with a technique called Somatic Dream Experience™ and how it can be used to treat physical symptoms and pain.

Chapter 11 explores the power of *Waking Dreaming*™ and how to recognize the profound meaning of your daily experiences. You will learn to look through the lens of waking time just as you would view your nighttime dreams. Waking Dreaming™ embodies the importance of synchronicity, leading to heightened wakefulness while enhancing your nighttime dream recall and understanding. This unique process will expand your self-awareness, and personal and spiritual evolution.

The Addendum provides a useful Dream Analysis Template for working with your dreams. It is a simple, straightforward way to interpreting your dreams. This template is particularly popular with dreamers who desire to approach dreams quickly. It is a user-friendly process for engaging in self-inquiry and thoroughly uncovering your dream's unique message.

DREAMS

By Mary Oliver, American poetess

All night
the dark buds of dreams
open richly.

In the center
of every petal
is a letter,
and you imagine
if you could only remember
and string them all together
they would spell the answer.

It is a long night,
and not an easy one—
you have so many branches,
and there are diversions—
birds that come and go,
the black fox that lies down

to sleep beneath you,
the moon staring
with her bone-white eye.

Finally you have spent
all the energy you can
and you drag from the ground
the muddy skirt of your roots
and leap awake
with two or three syllables
like water in your mouth
and a sense
of loss—a memory
not yet of a word,
certainly not yet the answer—
only how it feels
when deep in the tree
all the locks click open,
and the fire surges through the wood,
and the blossoms blossom.

CHAPTER ONE

The numinous nature of your nighttime dreams

Dreams are a sacred gift presented to us in the midst of our sleeping consciousness. Remember your dreams. Honor your dreams. Learn from your dreams.

—Norman Bradford

Dreams are alive. Rich with symbols, archetypes, alchemical images, and metaphors, dreams are an invaluable transformational instrument. When understood, dreams are a pathway to higher consciousness, evolved relationships, meaningful work, informed physical health, and a clear awareness of your soul's blueprint. But the growth that dreams provide is not always an easy process, it sometimes requires digging into unconscious muck which makes things appear messy. Also, unhealed trauma rears its head during dreamtime as do addictions, fears, unrequited love, grief, disappointment, anger, and physical, psychological, and spiritual imbalances. The unconscious does its best to grab your attention so you can recognize and integrate aspects of yourself that are hidden and may have gotten repressed along the way. Further, dreams possess the power to free you from programmed beliefs, status quo thinking, and false personas. They provide ideas, solutions, and insights. Edgar Cayce taught, "Dreams work to solve problems of the dreamer's

1

conscious waking life, and they work to quicken in the dreamer new potentials which are his/hers to claim."

Dreams are considered to be the oldest language known to man and some are *numinous* in nature, a term Jung used frequently when referring to their "divine command" (derived from the Latin word *numen*). These watershed experiences encompass significant health-related issues, profound relationship matters, vocational and career crossroads, and spiritually defining moments. Dreams emerge from the point of contact between spirit and matter, human and divine, male and female, ego and Self. Carl Jung calls this point of contact the *soul*. Since your dreams provide ideas, solutions, and insights, I encourage you to use this book as your own personal compass for navigating through every area of your life. Literally, they are jackpots of information and will enhance your awakening process, or what Jung called the pathway to individuation.

Dreams are sacred gifts; no matter how confusing, nonsensical, frightening, or perverse they may seem, *dreams emerge from the unconscious to help you.* We often avoid facing a disturbing or puzzling dream but in truth it is your own personal *daimon*, the Greek word for "inspired guide."

My dream work combines depth psychology and somatic practices and focuses on four basic principles developed by Carl Jung:

1) Almost every dream come to us in the service of health and wholeness.
2) Dreams have multiple and simultaneous meanings.
3) Only the dreamer knows for sure what the meaning of the dream is at a particular time.
4) Dreams bring information from the unconscious into consciousness.

Informing these principles is the universality of certain motifs which Jung calls "archetypes." All four of the basic principles are applicable to the personal growth of the individual and to the health and wholeness of the culture. In addition, dreams offer special gifts which help you with the following issues.

Discover and reclaim your shadow

Your shadow contains aspects of you that are unconscious or that you may have judged as "negative" or "bad." (And also include positive traits that you have not yet acknowledged or accepted.) Discovering your shadow allows you to become aware of all aspects of self which leads to integration, wholeness, and individuation. Jung viewed the individuation process as our ultimate goal. Individuation requires becoming conscious of our *prima materia*—the unconscious material that has been repressed so we may experience the alchemical process of transformation. Dreams provide the opportunity to witness the *prima materia* in ways that we are unable to experience during waking life. People who advance towards individuation tend to become harmonious, mature, responsible, and are aware of their connectedness to all things.

Jung stated, "The commonest dream symbol of transcendence is the snake." A personal example entails a series of "snake" dreams I began having when I immersed myself in a program grounded in depth psychology and somatic studies. As I delved into the hidden realms of the unconscious, childhood trauma, and attachment theory, "snake" dreams began to emerge. Having been terrified of snakes my entire life, I was confused about why they were showing up *now*? Were they trying to convey some aspect of me (a thought that horrified me), or were they representing someone in my life (almost as frightening)?

I sought advice from an instructor I deeply respected who advised, "Snakes sometime appear in dreams when there's a misalignment in psyche. You're on a new path that is triggering some old stuff, so write down your dreams and notice if they shift as you work through the course material." So I did. His advice was spot-on because the more I delved into the realm of the unconscious, the more snake surfaced during dreamtime. The more I remembered and re-witnessed childhood trauma, a myriad of snakes showed up—from black snakes with long red tongues to green diamondback rattlers. Somatic memories surfaced from the abuse and neglect I experienced during my developing years. This was the *prima materia* that had been buried and needed to surface so it could be reexperienced in a safe environment and transformed. Remaining dedicated to understanding my dreams and working with a somatic trauma therapist helped my snake dreams shift. As I moved through the trauma, "snake" evolved from something painful and frightening to an image that became my most powerful guide.

The body remembers everything you have ever experienced and carries the burden of stress, disease, and trauma. Dream images, like my myriad snakes, live in the blood cells, skin, muscles, and organs of the body. By working with the images, the snakes became my personal daimon to the point that even the "poison" that flooded my body after one snake decided to sink his fangs into my left hand became a form of "medicine." After the initial shock wore off, I was able to tap into the venom and receive the strength that I needed to confront the past and transform some painful experiences. This ancient, reptilian image led me to a deeper understanding about my reactions, behaviors, fears, and desire for love, and in alchemical terms, was akin to turning base metal into radiant gold. Using dream images to transform old wounds leads us to individuation, wholeness, and greater aliveness. You may be wondering, *what happened to the snake dreams?* Well, two weeks before finishing my final doctoral course and writing my last term paper, snake exited the realm of my dreams and hasn't made an appearance since.

Recognize your limiting patterns

By recognizing your limitations, you heighten your self-awareness and awaken to the realms of mystery and soul. Since dreams emerge from the unconscious and speak the language of the soul, whenever you pay attention to the deeper message in your dreams, you enhance your connection to soul. Playwright and novelist, Marsha Norman, once wrote, "Dreams are illustrations from the book your soul is writing about you." "Soul" differs from "spirit." James Hillman, an American psychologist who studied at the C. G. Jung Institute in Zurich explains how "spirit is fast" and ascends in a vertical direction. He compares it to a straight arrow, "knife sharp, powder dry, and phallic." In contrast to spirit, he speaks of the soul and its connection to the moon, the realm of the dead and dreams of the night. Soul can be experienced in the muddy, mucky waters we must sometimes wade through in life and the messiness that comes with growth. Our dreams speak soul-language which is why they are not easy to understand. Soul communicates with images that are imbued with importance and symbolism. Like poetry, in order to relish it we must dip beneath the surface and dive into its deeper meaning. Emerson once said, "Every *word* was once a poem" and this is true with dreams; every image was once a story of the soul.

A personal example of how dreams reveal our limiting patterns and awaken us to our highest potential is illustrated in a dream I had while going through a significant reinvention. For some clarity and support, I enlisted the help of a professional coach. After our first session, I had the following dream:

> *My coach and I are standing near the bottom of a hill that leads upward to*
> *a road. The hill is covered in snow. I am holding a silver ring with a large*

diamond in my right hand and I am not sure where it came from. A man
pulls up in a car on the road above us and gets out. He is holding a small
black pistol and is pointing it toward me. I am frightened and decide to
hide the ring by pushing the diamond end into the snowy bank in front
of us. My coach says something to the man. He puts his gun away and
I am relieved yet concerned about finding the ring I just hid in the snow.

Issues of prosperity, self-worth, and the shadow and light side of my
masculine aspects emerge from this dream. Let's unpack this dream:

- Snow covered hill: frozen emotions, unconscious perceptions, thoughts and feelings.
- Ring: connection with source, infinity.
- Diamond: multi-faceted, strong, beautiful, valuable, inner gifts and talents.
- Man with gun: masculine shadow aspect, threatening, challenging my self-worth regarding my ability to create prosperity.
- Coach: masculine light aspect, wise, supportive, fearless.

During my first coaching session we discussed the responsibility that
comes with success and prosperity. I shared my belief that in order to
generate success, I would have to give up my freedom and slave away all
day long. Wealthy, successful people must be workaholics and though
I was willing to exert positive energy, I was unwilling to "sacrifice"
my happiness. This dream was a gift from psyche that clearly exposed
the sacrificial belief living in the depths of my unconscious. Here are the
pearls of wisdom:

1. The dream begins with me standing at the bottom of a small hill
   that leads upward to a road. The hill symbolizes the effort I believe
   is required to overcome some repressed prosperity issues. Since the
   road is visible from the bottom of the hill, the issues I am facing are not
   insurmountable and my ability to overcome them are within reach.
2. I am holding a silver ring with a large diamond and unsure where it
   came from. The diamond ring represents my strength and multifaceted capacity for creating prosperity but am unaware that it's okay to
   claim it as mine.
3. I am afraid I am going to be hurt by the man with the gun who might
   steal my ring. The gunman is the conflicted part of me, challenging
   my self-worth for deserving abundance.

4. I push the ring into the snow bank. Snow reflects frozen emotions and some unconscious fears I am carrying.
5. My coach talks to the man which causes the man to put away his gun. This reveals the wise, intuitive aspect, the "voice of reason" reminding me of my abilities.
6. The dream concludes with a concern for having hid the ring so well I may be unable to recover it. Here again, issues of self-worth and sabotaging my success are being exposed.

"Until you make the unconscious conscious," Jung wrote, "it will direct your life and you will call it fate." This dream brought unconscious belief patterns into my awareness so I could address them. That's why dreams are so powerful; they continuously communicate messages from our unconscious to our conscious mind. This is also why we often resist remembering or working with them! We don't wish to see how clearly they reveal the truth about our vain imaginings and fragile ego self-concepts; dreams bust them apart.

Resolve problems in your relationships and face fears of intimacy

Relationships are a significant part of our lives. Jean-Paul Sartre stated, "Hell is other people," and though that might feel true at times, without relationships, we severely limit our ability to evolve. Humans are hardwired to connect. Developing open, loving, trusting, and healthy connections takes great commitment, consistent effort, and mindful awareness. Specific dream characters, symbols, and feelings emerge to show you unresolved fears, insecurities, and even traumatic experiences that occurred and are inhibiting your connection with others.

See your beliefs, attitudes, and judgments toward yourself and others

Dreams are often referred to as the "mirror to your soul" because they reflect the deeper, hidden aspects of us that we are not seeing clearly. Also, they reveal how others see us which likely differs from our self-perception. Jung referred to this aspect as the "persona," the mask we wear in public for others to see. It is the false-self that needs approval and strives to be liked, appreciated, and wanted. Therefore, our dreams are not meant to please us but to awaken us. They are often perceived as disturbing because they will not succumb to our noblest notions of ourselves. "The closer one looks," Marc Ian Barasch (2000) states, "The more [dreams] seem to insist upon a challenging proposition: You must live truthfully. Right now. And always. Few forces in life present, with an equal sense of inevitability, the bare-knuckle facts of who we are, and the demands of what we might become."

Identify warnings

Dreams reveal when someone has deceived you, when you may be in danger, and when your body is tired, run down, or sick. They can also show you what your body needs in order to heal. For years, I've had recurring dreams of my beloved dog being in danger, whether running into the street or getting lost. I am always trying to save her. Sometimes I am successful and other times I am not. It took me a couple of years to recognize a pattern: Every time I am out of balance from not getting enough rest, overindulging in sweets, or pushing myself too hard, this dream rears its head. Now when my dog appears and I am trying to rescue her, I know it is time to step up the self-care!

Create abundance in your life

When was the last time you found money or jewelry on the ground in a parking lot or on a sidewalk? Was it a penny, nickel, quarter, a dollar, or a twenty dollar bill? Did you pick it up and keep it, or walk away from it? Finding (or losing) valuables in dreams is symbolic of discovering (or losing) something of value in you. Locating valuables implies that you may be discovering something new within yourself, such as a new attitude, a new form of work, a new relationship, new prosperity, new creativity, and so forth.

Here is a personal example of how your dreams can provide specific direction for accessing your life's work and creating abundance. Years ago, I was a human resource director for a Certified Public Accountant and consulting firm in the Midwest. The majority of my time was spent firing managers and partners as the firm underwent a series of mergers. As a highly sensitive person and empath, this was excruciatingly painful and I experienced immense burnout in only a few short years. The life force had been sucked out of my soul and I resigned. Instead of immediately putting myself back on the executive market, I felt guided to take a year off and do some significant soul-searching. So I withdrew my 401(k) pension, bought a house on a small lake in the Midwest, and took my ten-year-old daughter, Alexis, and our cat, Buttercup, and moved in with my beloved partner, Thomas. It was a new beginning, both emotionally and financially challenging, yet I spent the next twelve months delving into spiritual teachings, journaling my thoughts and feelings, and working with my nighttime dreams. At thirty-two years old, it may have been one of the best years of my life.

Daily, I asked for guidance from my dreams and how best to use my gifts, strengths, and talents. During this time, I had a powerful dream:

> *I am sitting in the driver's seat of my red Toyota which is parked in a parking lot. Next to me in the passenger's seat I see a dark blue book with "Bhagavad Gita" scrolled in gold across the cover. I open the car door and see several brochures that I have created lying on the ground and next to them are various silver and gold coins.*

This dream was showing me that writing combined with spirituality were a definite part of my life's work. As I followed my dream's cues I began writing articles for spiritual and personal growth publications, something I had never done before. As a result, I had the following dream:

> *I am guided to look under my bed and discover enormous diamonds in the shape of crystals. I am amazed by their beauty. After looking under the bed I look to the floor and see two or three similar stones, not quite as large as the one under my bed. I awake feeling happy and inspired.*

These dreams affirmed the work that carried me deeper into my authentic self while providing abundance, not just financially, but emotionally, intellectually, creatively, and spiritually. The fact that the diamonds were shaped like crystals revealed the multifaceted potentials within me. Looking back over the past couple of decades, I can see how telling the dream truly was. I became inspired to write a series of articles that were published throughout the country and eventually morphed into my first book, *Gifts of the Soul*. Next, the book and articles inspired the creation of The Self-Mastery Program, an intensive course that supported individuals in accessing their inner gifts. I taught

The Self-Mastery Program for ten years and in the meantime, penned my second book, *The Intimate Soul*. (Both books were written and self-published under my former name, Laura V. Hyde.)

Unlimited ideas continued to spring forth and I developed a series of additional programs, workshops, and retreats. During this creative era, I generated a course on dreams and coached people on understanding and utilizing them. Desiring to deepen my spiritual growth, I attended an interfaith seminary program and began providing spiritual counseling.

The "multifaceted" diamonds represented skills I never knew I had, and didn't have, until I began working with my nighttime dreams and stretching beyond my comfort zone. Edgar Cayce wisely affirms, "Dreams are today's answers to tomorrow's questions." Listen to your dreams. Like a diamond, they possess marvelous, mystical, multifaceted brilliance.

Why is sleep so healing?

And if tonight my soul may find her peace in sleep, and sink in good oblivion, and in the morning wake like a new opened flower then I have been dipped again in God, and new created.

—D. H. Lawrence

We spend a great amount of time sleeping. In fact, statistics reveal that one-third of our lives is spent asleep. That means by the time you reach sixty, you will have spent approximately twenty years asleep. Out of those years, you will have spent 87,000 hours actively dreaming. Imagine how many dreams you have throughout your lifetime. And just think of all of the wisdom, ideas, and creative genius pouring forth from your subconscious, the place within you where your experiences and knowledge is stored. American author and Quaker, Jessamyn West, once penned, "Sleeplessness is a desert without vegetation or inhabitants."

Sleep is essential in order for our bodies to rejuvenate. In 2013, researchers at the University of Rochester in New York discovered that the brain sweeps away waste and toxins during sleep. That is why the cats or kids keeping waking you up at night, or drinking that second glass of wine, or experiencing hormonal changes cause you to feel foggy the next day. The flow of cerebrospinal fluid increases dramatically in the brain during sleep, cleaning out toxins which could lead to certain diseases like Alzheimer's. While you are sleeping, your brain cells shrink by sixty percent, allowing waste to be reduced more effectively. Restful, non-interrupted sleep is essential. Keep your room dark and cool, turn on some white noise like a fan, wear ear plugs and a sleep mask if necessary, but make sure you get a good night's sleep.

Not only does restful sleep enable your conscious mind to take a break, it allows the unconscious mind to fulfill an important function: to recreate the conscious mind's desire for depositing and permanently housing one's experiences. These remain until the experience or belief has been changed or reprogrammed. As the experiences are deposited into the unconscious, we act according to what has been stored—whether we are conscious of it or not. Sleeping is perhaps one of the greatest gifts we can give ourselves. "Put your thoughts to sleep," Rumi once advised, "Do not let them cast a shadow over the moon of your heart. Let go of thinking." Sleep possesses the capacity to restore us emotionally, physically, intellectually, creatively, and spiritually.

Dreaming and dream recall

Dreams come to us and we remember them when we are ready to get it …
the fact they're coming to us means we're ready.

—Robert Johnson

Are you able to remember your dreams? If so, how many dreams do you recall? Many factors affect dream recall including medication, stress, alcohol, food, illness, how many hours you sleep, how deeply you sleep, and, of course, fear of recall. You might wonder: *Why on earth would I be afraid to remember my dreams?* There are many reasons including feeling uncomfortable or afraid about things we don't understand or wish to face within ourselves. Also, we tend to invalidate the unknown. I have witnessed this many times while being interviewed about dreams on radio or TV. Inevitably, one person will challenge: "What research shows that dreams mean anything at all!?" Responding to such a question is impossible; it's akin to the old saying: "The atheist can't find God for the same reason that a thief can't find a policeman."

Dreams are meant to help you, not harm you, and that includes the disturbing poisonous diamondback rattlesnake trying to bite you as much as the radiant golden chalice given to you by a loving, wise woman.

And again, we dream every night whether we remember our dreams or not. Rather than asking someone, "Did you have any dreams?" Try this: "Do you remember any of your dreams from last night?"

The art of dream recall is like anything else you want to experience: You must have the *desire* to remember them. Dream images often live in the shadows and if they haven't been acknowledged or tended to in a long while (or, ever), they need some gentle coaxing. The more you seek to understand them, the more likely you will recall them.

Total recall in seven steps

1. Set your intention to remember your dreams before falling asleep. Before falling asleep, repeat three times: "Tonight I'm going to remember my dreams." Tell your dream self that you are willing to remember your dreams, even if it's only a small "snippet." Like anything else in life, what we place our attention on expands and dream recall is no different. Dreams may seem silly but only to your waking mind. Often people who cannot remember their dreams are resistant for various reasons. This is understandable considering how confusing and frightening they might seem. Again intention and action are key; it is impossible to trick psyche, you are either committed to remembering your dreams or you are not.

2. Keep a dream journal near your bed (or a tape recorder). The more you record your dreams, the more dream recall you will experience. Writing the dream down anchors it and demonstrates your commitment enabling you to progress from the mental level of intention to the physical level of action. The other important reason for recording your dreams is that you will have clearer recall upon awakening. If you wait to write them down, you risk losing the clarity of the dream including the *feelings* you experienced while having the dream, and your feelings are essential. Dreams are elusive and will disappear within seconds.

3. Pose a question before falling asleep. It may pertain to any area of your life in which you would like some guidance. Allow any issues you are working on, or answers you are seeking, to come into your awareness as you fall asleep. Ask one question about a situation you are dealing with and have trust that your dreams will give you the answer(s). The issue isn't to try to control the outcome of your dreams, so only ask open-ended questions.

4. Record your dreams as soon as possible, even if it's during the night. Try not to turn on any bright lights or anything that makes noise. Turning on an overhead light may take you out of a state of dream awareness and cause you to lose the dream completely. Using a light-pen works wonders. Always record the dream using the first person narrative "I" and in the present tense. The key is to keep yourself in the dream so you can recall as much as possible. You want to feel the dream as though it is alive, a living embodied experience that lives inside of you. Record even the smallest bits and pieces of your dream, they could very well be the catalysts for remembering the rest of the dream later in the day. Even writing down a snippet of your dream is helpful and often triggers the ability to recall the rest of the dream.

5. *Carpe noctem!* If you awake during the night, seize the opportunity by focusing on what you want, for example, guidance about a specific issue, desire, or interest. Instead of worrying about your finances, health, or "to do" list at 3a.m., choose what you center your energy on. Think about something in your life you would like to enhance; it could entail your work, health, or family. What you shine your light of attention on will often manifest as a dream when you fall back to sleep. I practice this regularly and have received dreams flowing with guidance about sensitive relationship issues, ideas for juicing up my creative projects, and even specific foods to add to my diet for increasing energy.

6. Focus on dream symbols and feelings while recording your dream. Recall the feelings you had during the dream and upon awakening, but be careful not to judge your dream. Remember that the majority of dreams are metaphoric, not literal. People tend to think the worst about their dreams, which blocks their ability to understand them. Again, dreams are given to us to *help* us become more aware.

7. Make a commitment to remember your dreams and develop your own "dream language." As you do so, your dreams will become easier to remember and understand. Dreams are recalled within seconds upon waking so you may have only fifteen to twenty seconds to "upload" a dream into your long-term memory banks. Your dream journal will become a valuable tool as you proceed on your soul's adventure.

Put it into practice!

- Practice remembering your nightly dreams by asking for guidance and insight about a situation. The goal is not to control your dream state but to open the door for your soul to openly communicate.
- Set your intention before going to bed and be specific about your willingness to remember your dreams and to receive guidance.
- Write down any dreams immediately upon waking and reflect on them throughout the day. Pay attention to the landscape, feelings, colors, odors, body sensations, and any dream images that "call" to you, especially disturbing ones. You might want to use a recording device with a night-light so you do not have to turn on the light which can interfere with dream recall and your ability to fall back asleep.

CHAPTER TWO

Common dream themes

Dreams are the guiding words of the soul. Why should I henceforth not love my dreams and not make their riddling images into objects of my daily consideration?

—Carl Jung

Dream symbols are *very* personal. And as I mentioned in Chapter 1, dreams have multiple meanings and only the dreamer truly knows the meaning of a dream. You and I may both dream about a "baby," but because you are starting a new project, your "baby" might reflect giving birth to an idea you feel passionate about. Yet, because I am exploring the realm of my inner child, my "baby" could represent Jung's "Sacred Child" archetype. So I avoid using "dream symbol books" to understand one's dreams.

However, that being said, there *are* certain topics that appear more often than others. You may think you're the only one dreaming of trying to find a bathroom or being pursued by a shadowy figure, but you are not. Dream research shows that there are several types of dream themes that people experience at one time or another. How do dream themes lead to awakening? They reveal invaluable visual metaphors for our emotional and psychological development. Though they might appear universal in meaning, they possess significant value that is personal to you, the dreamer. A few of the most common dream themes encompass: vehicles, bridges, animals, baby, bathrooms, being chased, classroom and taking a test, death, falling, fire, Eros/sex, flying, houses/ buildings, landscapes, nudity, and water. Let's address a few common themes starting with vehicles.

Why are vehicles in dreams significant?

Vehicles are the way we move from one place to another. And in dreams, vehicles have the capacity to represent how our soul uses our body to travel through life. There are many different kinds of vehicles, but for practical purposes, we're going to focus on those that typically appear.

Who is in the driver's seat?

Regardless of the type of vehicle, it's always important to notice who is navigating. Whether it is a sailboat, car, bus, or train, the driver in your dream is always the one in control. Being any other place than in the driver's seat implies that you are not in charge of your life. Perhaps you are drifting aimlessly, or maybe you are allowing yourself to be controlled by another. The point is, you are meant to be the one driving your life. In fact, it's really the only thing you have control over, your life, no one else's.

When a vehicle appears in your dream, notice where you're sitting. If someone other than you is in the driver's seat, who is it? This person is the one presently in control of your life. This is true even if they are deceased. How can that be? Well, it can occur if you're living your life according to someone else's idea of how your life should be, or, if you're operating in a way that subscribes to someone else's belief system, standards, and criticisms. This is often symbolized by an authority figure who was influential and controlling in your life—and still is—even though you may be an adult. This issue arises from the fact that we may have been criticized by adults while growing up. Our minds take that criticism and create the infamous and destructive Inner Critic or Bully.

If you're not in control of the vehicle, your dream is bringing this fact to light so you can change. The dream will usually reveal who is in control. The type of vehicle shows you the area(s) and intensity at which it is occurring. For example, a student of mine once dreamt the following dream about being in a car with her family of origin:

I am sitting in the back seat of a large, crowded car. My childhood family members are packed in the car, sister, mother, and grandmother who is actually deceased. My older brother is driving and my father is sitting in the passenger's seat. We come upon a flooded bridge and the car cannot cross the river. Suddenly the car careens out of control and off the road! Everyone exits the car and we begin walking.

First, note that the dreamer recorded the dream in the *first person* and *present tense*. Writing down your dreams from this place keeps the dream vivid in psyche, body, and soul. It places you *inside* the dream where feelings, perceptions, and sensory experiences remain alive. Archetypal psychologist, James Hillman, once affirmed: "When I look at a dream in the morning, it is like a picture … but when I am in the dream at night, it is like a scene. I'm actually in it, I'm moving around in it. The landscape is three-dimensional, as though I am inside the dream."

Second, the dreamer is not driving, her older brother is. Her father is also sitting up front. Where is the dreamer sitting? In the backseat along with her family members including her grandmother. The dreamer might be allowing her brother's beliefs and to a lesser extent, her father's attitudes, to be in charge of her life. These attitudes and beliefs are causing her to feel out of control about her life. Perhaps she felt controlled by her brother and father in her family when she was younger, or maybe she experienced some trauma as a result of living in an environment that was out of control. Unresolved trauma will appear in your nightly dreams. (Trauma will be discussed later in the book.)

As we look more closely at the dream, we notice that the men are sitting up front, which may reveal the dreamer is allowing more "masculine" beliefs and behaviors to run the show. Masculine behaviors focus on doing, being assertive, making things happen, etc., while in the backseat are the females and a "feminine" set of beliefs which suggests being, listening, trusting, intuiting, etc. The dreamer may be downplaying her feminine aspect so it is taking a "back seat" in her life. However, the masculine approach is causing her to feel out of control and in danger so the dream may be telling her to become aware of the imbalance in her life so she can reclaim her inner power.

Automobiles

Cars represent the body and/or your lifestyle. Your automobile reflects your physicality in its current condition as well as the attitude you have about your body and yourself. The type of car, color and size are important for your dreams have the ability to show you if, and where, your body is in need of healing.

When your own automobile appears, it indicates the way you travel through life; your desires, accomplishments, the way you see yourself, the pace at which you travel. Other makes of automobiles may reveal your state of mind including a need for more freedom (racing car), a yearning for fun (sports car/convertible), feelings of being overwhelmed and even how you're feeling about the work you do (semi-trucks or trucks carrying heavy loads of stuff).

If your vehicle appears scratched, smashed, or in need of repair, it might be revealing low self-esteem, how you're currently treating yourself, and the condition of your body. Maybe it's time to add more exercise into your daily routine. Or, perhaps, your diet needs to be replaced with one that is healthier and more nourishing. When your car appears damaged in any way, it's time to pay particular attention to the health of your body. I teach my students if you have more than one dream about a damaged car, pay particular attention to your health and seek medical counsel.

1. Battery

The battery in a car represents motivation and energy. A dead battery might be a warning that you are low on energy and need to be "recharged." Look at your life and notice if you are feeling burned out. Perhaps you need to take a break and step back from your daily routine and relax. Or, you might need to eliminate something or someone that is draining your energy. *New York Times* best-selling author Dr. Judith Orloff has written books and taught classes on what she calls "emotional vampires," people who suck your energy because they're not dealing with their own issues. If you work or live with someone who zaps your exuberance, don't be naïve, take action toward setting strong boundaries and do what it takes to protect your precious life-force energy.

2. Engine

Engine represents power, strength, energy, and stamina. Like a failed battery, engine failure may be a sign for you to get a "tune-up" and replenish your body, mind, and spirit. I once had the following dream:

I am driving my yellow BMW M Roadster down a freeway and notice that
an engine light appears. It is a triangle with an exclamation point inside.
"That's strange, I've never seen that before," I think, but continue driving.
Then I push a button to turn on the radio so I can listen to my favorite talk
show program but it doesn't work.

The following morning, I check my car and everything is fine. I inspect
the car's owner's manual and find the exact engine light that appeared
in the dream and it says "malfunction" but it does not specify what
kind of failure. Since I am scheduled to depart for a road trip, I take
my car into the BMW dealer. They diagnose that there is virtually no
"charge," my alternator needs to be replaced and that my car would
likely break down the next time I drove it. If I had ignored my dream,
I could have been in real danger. The very next day I was scheduled to
drive from San Luis Obispo to Santa Monica, California on Highway
101 and my car could have shut down in the middle of the freeway.
Heed the wisdom of your dreams!

3. Headlights

Headlights allow us to see at night, and in your dreams, headlights represent your ability to see things clearly. Here is a good rule of thumb:
light = awareness. For example, if only one headlight is working it
might mean you are unaware that something important is happening.
No headlights, well, that's pretty obvious—you're truly in the dark!
You may be in denial about a circumstance, afraid to look at something,
or disassociating from your feelings or "blacking out." Expanding our
awareness entails integrating the unconscious aspects of ourselves into
consciousness. Headlights working or not working reveal something
that is trying to be seen, but for various reasons we are unable or unwilling to shine the light on it. Journaling about concerns you may have,
or discussing them with a trusted friend or partner will help you
heighten your awareness and see the light.

Buses

Buses are another type of vehicle that frequently appear during dreamtime. Buses transport large groups of people and are a common and inex-
pensive means of travel. Buses imply "taking the road most traveled,"

non-original thinking, following others' ideas and viewpoints, and adhering to the status quo. If a bus appears in your dream, ask yourself, "Am I following my heart? Am I living my life in a way that works for me? Do I give my power away by being attached to what others think of me? What is happening right now that is causing me to seek the approval of another, and who is that person?"

Boats

Boats are made for the water and since water symbolizes your emotions and spiritual growth, boats are related to your spiritual side. Some boats, like cruise ships, may imply a need for vacation or fun, while sailboats reveal skimming the surface of your subconscious. Since sailboats, unlike powerboats, are powered by nature (the wind), they reveal a deeper state of consciousness and faith. Whether or not you're sailing smoothly is key, of course. Rowboats imply that you are struggling through life and going the hard way, while paddleboats show that you are using your own strength and power and are self-sufficient.

Planes

Aircraft are unique in that they travel the fastest of all vehicles. When an airplane shows up in your dreams, it means you are rising above the situation and that you are a free thinker. How high you are flying is important for it shows you how far "above" the situation you are. It also reveals your mental state of awareness and how quickly you're moving on the inner planes. Airplanes, when flying smoothly, show that you are growing and with ease. This type of vehicle denotes your attitudes, thoughts, and feelings on the "mental planes."

Put it into practice!

Check your dream journal and focus on any vehicles mentioned. Take a few moments to answer the questions below.

- What kind of vehicle is it?
- Who is driving/flying/sailing the vehicle?
- Where are you located in the vehicle?
- What is the condition of the vehicle?
- Where is the vehicle taking you?

Are you able to see how your dream vehicle is helping you learn how you're choosing to travel through life?

Bridges: gateways to growth

Another common dream theme is a bridge. Bridges are powerful symbols because they connect us, or "bridge" into another level of consciousness. A student once shared his dream about a "toll bridge":

> *I am walking toward a huge bridge that crosses over a large body of water ... ocean? I can't tell because it is dark outside but I am excited about crossing the bridge. As I get closer to the bridge, I see a woman sitting on a small stool and she is wearing a black cape and the hood is covering her hair and face. As I approach her, she sticks out her hand and I realize I have to pay a toll in order to cross the bridge. I am curious about what she looks like, then she pulls off her hood and I see that it is a woman that I have seen before and am very attracted to. She has long, wavy auburn hair and a beautiful face. She informs me that if I pay the toll, she will tell me what I need to know to cross the bridge. I give her some coins then she whispers something to me that I know is very important. When I awake I cannot remember what she told me and feel frustrated.*

Dreams of bridges, like the one the dreamer shared, are very important. If a "bridge toll keeper" appears, they often have a covered face, yet, they can offer us great guidance so pay attention to this figure. In this particular dream, the woman taking the bridge toll shared something with the dreamer that may have been essential to the dreamer in order for him to move to another level of consciousness. She may have been the dreamer's "anima" which is his female aspect (women dream of the "animus" which represents our masculine aspect), or, she could have been a mythical figure or siren that wanted to capture the attention of the dreamer. Either way, she had something important to impart for the dreamer's growth and individuation. The fact that he could not remember her words of wisdom may indicate that he was afraid or resisting the information. After all, once we know what we know we can never go back.

Baby

Interestingly, both women and men can dream of being pregnant and giving birth to a baby. I've had male students share pregnancy dreams and whether you are a man or a woman, being pregnant or holding a baby often signifies a new beginning, project, or creative aspiration. (Note: Also, dreaming of a child may mean it's time to work with your inner child or the sacred child archetype.)

Being chased

This is a classic pursuit dream that can morph into a nightmare. Ask yourself, "Who or what is chasing me?" "What am I currently resisting in my life—a feeling, issue, problem?" "Am I running away from something I need to face?" This could be an addiction (which manifests in myriad forms including sex, drugs, prescription medications, food, alcohol, tobacco, exercise, shopping, working, relationships, perfection, gambling, stealing, video games, internet, TV), speaking your truth to someone, facing a fear, healing a relationship, confronting your shadow, and more. Many years ago, I used to dream of a man chasing me and trying to break into my bedroom window or front door. These dreams were incredibly frightening and it took a long while before I realized they were about the integration of my animus (male aspect). The "marriage" of the masculine and feminine is discussed in length in Chapter 5: "The hidden power of the anima, animus, and shadow."

Classroom/taking a test

This is one of the most common dream themes and they occur when we are feeling "tested" and/or not ready or prepared for an upcoming challenge or responsibility. I often have these kinds of dreams when I am preparing to teach, speak publicly, or embark on a new adventure. For example, on April 16, 2017, Easter Sunday, I had an anxiety-ridden dream of not being prepared to present at a spiritual community I was leading. The day before in waking life, I outlined the vision for a new inter-spiritual center I was planning on opening at the beginning of 2018. That night I had the following dream:

> I am in a woman's house on a Sunday morning when I realize that I am supposed to be speaking at my spiritual center. I feel completely unprepared. Other women are now in the house, giving me ideas for topics but I can barely hear them. I'm feeling desperate as I only have twenty minutes to get to the church so I get into a new white Jeep that the woman who owns the house drives.

I arrive at the church and hear music that is very powerful. I'm still upset and am trying to find a bathroom to get cleaned up. My husband approaches me and says, "I know what you can talk about, the body." *I think that is a wonderful idea because I will bring a somatic perspective into spirituality! Then I wake up and am very relieved it is a dream and not waking life.*

"Not feeling ready" is the core theme of this dream. As I previously mentioned, it emerged on the heels of opening a new spiritual center and my unconscious is letting me know I do not feel prepared. My difficulty in hearing the women speak points to not listening to my inner feminine wisdom because my anxiety is blocking my intuitive voice. The white Jeep is symbolizing a "rugged spirituality" and reflects how I can travel through this time of change but need to toughen up and face my fears. However, I am not in the driver's seat, I am a passenger, so I need to take ownership of my vision and remain grounded in it.

I could say more about this dream but the core theme is the "classroom" of my current vision and goals and "not feeling ready to pass the test." My husband's suggestion of talking about the "body" reflects what I am currently studying in my doctoral program and represents my present focus, not what I used to concentrate on at my former spiritual center.

Again, classroom and taking a test dreams are very common and often emerge during times of change, when you are preparing to "perform" in some way, and/or trying something new. When this dream theme occurs, take special note of the environment, the feelings, and how the dream ends for the ending reveals which way the energy in your life is moving.

Death

As frightening as dreams of death may seem, they could imply that something within you is dying out. It could be an attitude, belief, attachment to something or someone. What are you releasing or are you willing to let go of? I've had numerous dreams about death and in some of them, I have even died. Here is one I had a few years ago:

I am standing on the shore of the Pacific Ocean near my home. I watch with awe as the waves flow toward me and grow in size. The longer I watch, the larger the waves grow and I realize a tsunami is coming towards me.

The waves are crashing over me and I know I am going to drown and am
sad. At first I resist, but as I plunge deeper into the ocean I decide to let
go and surrender. The water begins to fill up my lungs and I know I am
dying. And yet, I am aware that my thoughts and consciousness are still
flowing as usual. My body is dead and it drifts to the floor of the ocean,
but the witness, or, "I Am" aspect of me continues to live, I feel okay then
awaken from the dream.

I felt comforted from knowing that part of me still existed even though
my body had drowned. Intuitively, I sensed this was an alchemical
dream representing unconscious aspects of me that were "stuck" and
in need of some fluidity for my development and individuation. From
a psychological perspective, I was experiencing an alchemical process
called *solutio*, one of the most significant processes in alchemy that
turns something solid into a liquid. The "solid" is something linger-
ing in our psyche that is in need of softening, understanding, healing,
or transforming. In this case, the immense water energy in dreamtime
was reflecting my detaching from someone that I had known for several years and was ready to release. But it went even deeper than that;
it revealed a transformation I was going through that tied into some of
my original attachments with my mother when I was an infant. When
we let go of our attachment to someone, it often triggers unconscious
attachment issues that occurred during our development years. This
can make "letting go" a very difficult thing to do. Releasing something
or someone can manifest as dreams of death.

Eros/sex

Eros is not the childish cupid image we've been taught but *creative life
energy*. Sigmund Freud believed that Eros was a masculine god, with
forward-moving energy that pulls us toward others (in a deep, engaging manner), towards the future, towards the new. Therefore, Eros
dreams may have several different meanings and can range from
repressed sexual energy to creatively expressing yourself. If you are
having sex with someone you know, notice who it is for the dream may
be revealing your wish to "connect" with the aspects this person represents to you. If you are having sex with someone you do not recognize, notice if it is a male or female for the dream may be showing

your desire to align with your feminine or masculine aspects. Do not be embarrassed or ashamed of any kind of sex dream! Your dreams are amoral; they are not interested in the rightness or wrongness of anything. Dreams of incest and/or having sex with friends, coworkers, bosses, ex-partners, and people of the same sex (if we're straight) or people of the opposite sex (if we're gay), are not meant to be taken literally. These dream themes are about our *desire to connect and integrate aspects of ourselves which the sexual dream character personifies*. Feelings of guilt will only prevent you from clearly seeing the message your dream is trying to convey.

Houses

Childhood homes, your current home or houses you have never lived in commonly appear in our dreams. Houses and buildings tend to reveal your current state of consciousness. Observe where you are in the house. Are you in the upper part of the home, on the main floor or in the basement? Climbing up the stairs toward the top of the house may signify growth and development in some area of your life, a rising in consciousness. Basements are important because they often represent the unconscious and can be dark and scary. If you dream about a childhood home, notice the age you were when you lived there and reflect on the beliefs and attitudes you had while living there. They could be the same attitudes and beliefs you are presently experiencing about a circumstance.

Houses and buildings can also represent the condition of your body, so if you dream about your house, pay attention to your physical health. Is there something in the house that is broken like a piece of furniture, or is the structure of the house in need of repair? Like automobile dreams, psyche may be alerting you to an underlying health issue.

Landscapes

Although landscapes are often ignored and misunderstood, they are very powerful and set the tone for the entire dream. Notice if you are indoors, outdoors, time of day or night, what kind of landscape appears, and how you feel about being in it. Dreams of being in the natural world are highly significant because the Earth is a living organism in which we are interconnected with all living things. Dreaming of the Earth can connect us to the doorway of our ecological self and psychic thoughts and feelings desiring to surface. And currently, as the environment shifts in dramatic ways, dreams of outdoor landscapes and natural disasters are becoming more common and being experienced individually and collectively. An example of a landscape dream is discussed in Chapter 3 under "The watery realm of emotional dreams."

Water

Water possesses the power to ignite an alchemical transformation. And transformation means change, change means letting go, and letting go requires some degree of grief. Water often depicts grief. I believe that we are greatly deprived of grief-work. Psychologist James Hillman, who studied with Carl Jung in the 1950s, delved deeply into dreams and believed so strongly in the need to keep our emotions balanced that he allowed himself to grieve thirty minutes every day. Water represents tears that need to be released. Emotional tears shed hormones and other toxins which accumulate during stress. Grieving during dreamtime is one way that psyche expresses itself so healing can occur. When water appears in your dreams, ask: "What emotional weight or burden am I carrying that needs to be released?"

Put it into practice!

- Dreams themes and symbols are personal to the dreamer. So even though I have given you some potential meaning for common dream themes, what matters most is what the dream symbol, image, or theme means to *you*.
- Notice if you experience one or more of the above common dream themes and pay attention to what is happening in your life when the dream appears. For example, taking a test will emerge through psyche when I am getting ready to speak publicly, host an event, or teach a class and am not feeling prepared. I might *believe* I am ready when I am awake, but then a dream of not having my notes available, or being unable to find the classroom will pop up and then

I know that despite my waking belief, another part of me is saying: "Consider a little more prep time!"
- Keep a list of common dream themes and notice when they appear and how they are guiding you in your waking life.

In the following chapter, we will visit specific "dream keys" to support your understanding of the power of your dreams and the particular meaning that is uniquely meant for you.

CHAPTER THREE

Decoding the language of your dreams

An uninterpreted dream is like an unopened letter from God.
—The Talmud

Six essential keys for opening the doorway to self-awareness

Dream Key #1: Dreams occur in sequence and build upon each other

Most of us average four to five dreams per night whether we remember them or not, and the first dream sets the tone for the rest of our dreams. As our dreams continue, they unfold and reveal deeper layers of *prima materia*. For example, if you are working on prosperity issues and desire to manifest more financial security or freedom, your first dream may involve something like finding valuables. It might be money or a purse that belongs to someone else. However, instead of feeling excited or contentment, you experience guilt. Then, as your dreams progress, your last dream of the night may involve your father and the environment he used to work in.

Upon waking you may feel confused: "What does any of this have to do with my father? And why did I feel guilty for finding valuables in my first dream?" Since dreams reveal the beliefs stored in your subconscious, these dreams may be showing you that you're not feeling deserving of being abundant and that your father didn't either. In fact, they may be reflecting the fact that he didn't like his job and had to sacrifice what he truly longed to do in order to make a living. If that were true, then you may have inherited the belief that it's not okay for you to do what you love to do *and* be prosperous. In this example, the first dream set the tone for the issue, but the last dream revealed the core problem, for example, the underlying belief that has been causing you to block the flow of abundance in your life.

Dream Key #2: Dreams are personal and meant for the dreamer

Every dream you have, except in rare cases, is meant for you. Since you're the dreamer, the dream reflects your perceptions, thoughts, and feelings, not someone else's—even if your dream seems to be about another person. There are exceptions to this dream key which entail two people who are closely connected. For example, my husband, Thomas, and I are great friends, life partners, and deeply connected on a soul level. We gave each other permission years ago to start our day by sharing our nighttime dreams. Dream themes encompass our kids, the natural world, our aging bodies, our sex life … and everything else that a human being on this planet might experience.

Thomas knows me better than anyone and occasionally he will have a dream that is meant for me. This rare occurrence happened recently:

> *Laura and I are at a conference. There's a number of notable people there, well-known spiritual teachers like Marianne Williamson, Jean Houston, and others. Some of the "famous" people speak and then it is Laura's turn. She hits a home run. The audience is very moved and they give Laura a standing ovation. The feeling I have is that Laura did a better job than the "famous" people. Marianne Williamson comes over to congratulate her and I feel very proud.*

Thomas dreamt this after we had had numerous discussions about opening a new spiritual center. We were both working through some concerns about my resuming the responsibility of being a spiritual leader when he had this dream. I had been asking my dream self for guidance and this dream affirmed that I was on the right track, yet it came through his psyche, not mine.

If you are connected in a significant and intimate way with someone, you may experience dreams for each other from time to time. When it happens, they are sacred gifts and deserve to be treated as precious treasures from the soul.

Dream Key #3: Everyone in the dream is an aspect of the dreamer ... most of the time ...

You might be dreaming about your partner being unfaithful or your boss being demanding, but every dream character represents some aspect of you. If mom was dominating and opinionated, then her presence in your dream may be saying that you are currently exhibiting these same behaviors. When someone appears, ask yourself, "What is my perception of this person?" It might be someone you haven't seen in twenty-five years or your current next door neighbor. The key is to get in touch with how *you* see this person and what traits they are mirroring back to you. This is not easy because no one wants to see negative qualities in themselves. Which is one of the reasons that the unlikeable traits have been projected on to another during dreamtime. Rich with self-awareness, dream characters are the psychic lens for you to truly see yourself. They reveal your false-self, the persona and mask that you wear as well as the traits you have adopted since you were very young. All those persons starring in your nightly dreams are unconscious projections of yourself. From this advantageous perspective, your dream characters can help you learn more about yourself than you might ever imagine.

Now, there are times when you are dreaming about someone and that person is playing him- or herself but this is only true in a couple of cases, for example, when you are in relationship with someone in which there are issues in need of attention. Perhaps there is unresolved conflict or tension that you are not aware of, or do not know how to address. Or, you've been asking for guidance about a particular relationship so the other person appears as him- or herself. In these examples, the dream may be illuminating the relationship dynamic between the two of you so you can begin to uncover the issues, patterns, obstacles that require attention.

The second case involves consciously telling your dream self that you want certain people to appear as themselves. This takes practice in order for it to work, so the best rule of thumb is to accept that most of the time, the characters appearing are aspects of you. Again, the most effective way to view dream characters through your own personal lens is to ask yourself, "What does this person represent to me? If I were to describe this person to someone, how might I depict them?" Since each of us sees through different lenses, based on our past experiences, certain people will appear in your dreams that have significant meaning only applicable to you.

A dream teacher once shared an interesting dream character tidbit about the Senoi who are the indigenous peoples of Peninsular Malaysia. They believed that if you dreamt about someone, you should make contact with them and let them know they appeared in your dream. My suggestion is to notice the connection you currently have with them. Is it congenial, positive, and healthy, or is it strained, conflicted, or estranged? The current tone of your relationship with the person is significant. If there are issues between you, then the dream may be guiding you to reach out and attempt to resolve the conflict. Perhaps taking responsibility or making an apology is needed and the dream is indicating it is the right time to do so. However, if the person appearing is someone you have not seen in many years, or are no longer in contact with, then the person is likely reflecting aspects of you. It is very important that we do not project our "stuff" onto another because it inhibits our ability to grow and evolve. But if the person appearing is ill, struggling, or suffering in any way, you may want to make it a point to check in with them and lovingly inquire as to how they are doing, *without* revealing how they appeared in your dream.

Dream Key #4: Dreams reflect your current life situation

While recording and working with your dreams, it is very helpful to recall what you were thinking and feeling the day before. What you experienced during the day is often the catalyst for what you dream that night. Your unconscious needs to "download" information, such as feelings, attitudes, perceptions, and so on, from the day. It's a quick and easy process of releasing pent-up energy while renewing as you sleep. It is also why strong emotions sometimes surface during dreamtime; sometimes we're not conscious of our feelings or able to comfortably express them. Thus our dreams are an avenue for releasing these feelings which allows us to "detox" our thoughts, feelings, and perceptions. Even if your dream is about something that happened five, ten, fifteen years ago, its desire is to reveal to you what is happening now, and how what may have happened in the past is affecting the present.

Dream Key #5: Every symbol is personal to the dreamer

Just as each dream character is an aspect of you and has significant meaning depending upon your beliefs, every dream symbol is relevant to you based upon your previous experiences. I am a writer, speaker, and teacher. Thus, when I dream about speaking in front of an audience, that would have a very different meaning to me than to someone who is uncomfortable speaking publicly. For example, the following dream from a client exemplifies the power of symbols:

> *I'm with a very old friend from high school and we're talking about sailing around the world. I look for a map and end up with a globe. We look at it and I tell him I've always wanted to sail directly west from where I live near the Pacific Coast in California. We look at the globe to see where that would take us and decide to do it and meet the next day. I check my phone and have a message from a potential new business client. I feel glad yet conflicted because I want the earnings but also want to go on this sailing trip.*
>
> *I'm now walking with a backpack towards a gas station where my old friend and I agree to meet. He's already there and his younger brother is with him. I'm glad to see his brother and assume he's going with us. My friend has a shiny, brand new car that he's fueling at the pump ... It is sporty and rugged looking and a spare tire is mounted on the front of the car. The tires seem to have zero miles on them and I ask, "Did you just get this? What year is it?" And my friend replies, "Yes, it's a special 2018 order."*

Several symbols emerge during this dream: map, globe, backpack, gas station, and a shiny car. Because my client has an affinity for sailboats, we began exploring this dream by tapping into what sailboats represent to him. "Freedom, lifestyle, spontaneity," are some of the descriptions he shared with me. This dream occurred near the beginning of 2017 and he was feeling torn between expanding his business practice and wanting to spend more time feeding his soul by engaging in creative projects. Because he perceived sailing and sail-related objects as his soul's desire to escape the confines of his daily work routine, we honed in on the globe, map, and backpack and the essences these dream symbols provided. Then we moved our attention to the shiny car and what it was trying to convey during dreamtime. For my client, the new car represented "lifestyle" choices and money. From this perspective, the car was an egoic, shiny diversion away from what his deeper self longed for, so the rest of our dream session focused on how my client could attain the essences that the sailing symbols represented in his life as it was at this point in time. His assignment was to gently detach from his inner critic's pressure to make more money while creating the time and space to experience what his soul was communicating through his dream.

Dream Key #6: Tonight's dreams can prepare you for tomorrow's experiences

Since I was sixteen, many of my nighttime dreams were foretelling of the following day's experiences. These are not the same as precognitive or psychic dreams but they are the pathway in which psyche speaks to us about the trajectory we will be taking the following day. Here is an example of such a dream:

> *I am outdoors with my beloved dog "Mia" and we are walking among the Live Oak and Sycamore trees on our property. Mia spots a family of wild turkeys and wants to play with them so she begins chasing after them. I call her to come to me but she is entranced by the turkeys and ignores me. Now there are cars driving down the road and I am afraid she is going to run into the road and get hit. I call her name more loudly and am running after her but she keeps chasing the turkeys. Mia runs farther away and I am no longer able to see her but I sense she is okay. I awake feeling concerned.*

My pets are precious to me and I am very protective of them. As I previously mentioned, dreams of my dog are quite frequently about "self-care," for example, taking extra good care of myself physically, emotionally, and spiritually. The day after I dreamt about Mia chasing the wild turkeys (which she loves to do in waking life!), I had two important deadlines to meet and one involved my dissertation proposal. Instead of starting my morning by journaling about my dreams and walking in nature, I began researching and writing, a bad way to begin my day. Before I knew it, my body was flooded with stress and cortisol, my heart rate was high, and I skipped eating breakfast and lunch.

Thankfully, as I was walking Mia along her favorite path later in the day I remembered the previous night's "Mia dream" and its vital warning: *tomorrow you will be tempted to overdo it and become imbalanced physically, emotionally and intellectually—be careful!* Although I wanted to keep pushing myself, I chose to listen to my body so I shut down my computer, grabbed a snack, and went for a long hike along the coast. By the time I returned, I was able to accept the fact that taking care of myself was more important than missing a deadline by one day. My unconscious had provided the necessary, loving warning I needed to remain balanced on several levels.

Dreams prepare us for challenges and opportunities that lie ahead. The more you work with your dreams, the more you will recognize repeated themes and symbols. These nocturnal leitmotifs emerge to support you in your journey, and if you pay attention they will guide you in creating healthy choices that nurture you physically, emotionally, intellectually, spiritually, and soulfully.

Deepening your dream understanding

Carl Jung declared: "Man's task is to become conscious of the contents that press upward from the unconscious." The unconscious most clearly reveals itself through our nighttime dreams because it is raw information uncensored by our conscious mind. Since dreams possess an infinite amount of wisdom, and though you may not believe you have sufficient time to work with every dream you remember, it is extremely beneficial to address dreams that are vivid, trigger deep feelings, and "call to you." You don't need to become a dream expert; you only need to record them and try to understand the incredible insight they offer. Here are some more tips for deepening your understanding.

First and foremost, do not judge your dreams—all dreams are significant and have much to tell you! Second, focus on feelings first, then dream symbols, then the theme of the dream. Third, there are different types of dreams so notice what realm of your life the dream is addressing:

- Physical
- Mental/issue-related
- Emotional
- Somatic
- Spiritual dreams.

Your inner physician in physical dreams

Physical dreams are fairly easy to recognize and are quite literal. For example, the buzzing of your alarm clock interferes with your sleep and you begin dreaming of a ringing telephone. Or, you're dreaming about having to go to the bathroom and in truth, you really need to get up and go! Physical dreams reveal the need to change your diet, release sexual energy, exercise, and receive medical attention. Physical dreams are often caused by physical noises and may also be prompted by physical environments: wind blowing on you, pets jumping on you, covers being pulled away from you leaving you cold.

When working with physical dreams, always look for a possible physical interpretation. Do not dismiss them as just silly dreams. Many times, certain dream symbols will appear which actually have a literal meaning. For example, dreams of cars or other vehicles and buildings often represent your body. If you dream of your car needing an overhaul, look to see if this applies to your body. Perhaps you are in need of a respite and the dream is warning you that one is needed or an illness may result.

This reminds me of a client I once worked with who had three recurring dreams of "broken plumbing" within her house. After having the second dream, she had her pipes checked out by a local contractor. Upon a thorough investigation she was told the plumbing in her house was fine. Then after the third recurring dream, she visited her physician and discovered that she had polyps in her colon, which if left untreated, could lead to colon cancer. After taking steps toward healing her colon, the dreams stopped and never returned. To this day, she is in excellent health and regularly uses her dream journal as her own "internal physician."

Physical dreams may appear in symbolic form such as the example with the plumbing, but the meaning directly relates to the condition of the body. They usually begin as "warning" signs and should not be ignored. This is especially true if you dream of your current car, or "rescue" vehicles such as a fire truck or ambulance. This also pertains to dreams of hospitals, doctors, medical treatment, or any symbol or scene that is "physically" related. (Please note: I discuss "healing dreams" again in Chapter 8.)

Physical dreams of death

Dreams of death often symbolize the "ending" of something: maybe a relationship, attitude, job, behavior, talent. However, there are certain symbols that represent a physical death and these include a stopped clock ("time has run out"), a river that has stopped flowing ("river of life"), a casket, your funeral, your will, or your tombstone.

A client who once had a drinking problem was courageous enough to share a dream of impending death with me: She saw a tombstone with her name on it and an empty vodka bottle on top of it. The symbolism was impossible to miss! This very short and succinct dream motivated her to seek counseling for some issues at the root of her alcohol abuse. Through therapy she was able to experience healing on all levels: physical, emotional, mental, and spiritual. Because of her commitment to healing she was able to transform her life and is now a successful healer who has helped countless people with her wisdom. Her willingness to understand her dreams was the springboard for a remarkable life.

Physical dreams vary and some may seem irrelevant, and some are. However, always take a few minutes to notice if there is a "physical warning" within the dream. If you're unsure, ask your dreams for guidance and trust any messages with a repeated dream theme. Physical dreams can be a powerful way to receive information about every part of your body.

Dreams of conflict in the mental sphere

Most of our dreams are issue related and fall under the category of "mental dreams." This is because the unconscious is working on areas of our lives where we are conflicted to some degree. The inner conflict might be relatively minor, as in how we can best get along with a difficult colleague, or it may be significant, as in whether or not we leave a job that pays well but is soul-sucking and leaves us feeling empty and depressed. Many of the dream examples in this book are mental/issue related dreams. These dreams are very important because they act as a compass in guiding us toward making choices, which builds integrity, character, inner strength, and honors our heart and soul. Dreams of this nature cover the full spectrum of relationships, career, financial security, self-esteem, social matters, and so forth. Here is an example of a dream my client had pertaining to infidelity:

I am out to dinner with my husband and want to connect with him but he is distracted. He keeps looking at a woman with long auburn hair at the next able. The more I try to get his attention, the more indifferent he becomes and I feel hurt.

*Now I am home and my husband has not returned from the restaurant.
I am afraid he is with the other woman. Then he walks in the door and lets me
know he is going back out for the night. He walks out the door and I pursue
him but am unable to turn the door knob. I keep trying to open the door but
the door knob breaks off in my hand. I awake feeling jealous and insecure.*

In some cases, dreaming about our partner being unfaithful is true as I
will discuss in the following example. But in certain situations, dreams
like this have nothing to do with infidelity or trust. My client has been
married for twenty-one years and has one of the healthiest and most
trusting marriages I've ever seen. She and her husband are able to openly
discuss their concerns and work them through with understanding and
love. When this type of dream rears its head it occurs when my client's
husband's workload is heavier than normal. And because of his work,
he may not be as emotionally available as she might prefer. So even
though she might awake and dart him the evil eye as he lays peacefully
sleeping, the dream is not literal.

However, it's vital we trust our intuition and do not dismiss dreams
as these as "not literal" because sometimes they are. A client once shared
a series of dreams she was having about her husband of nineteen years
that demonstrates this point:

*I'm on vacation with my husband and am getting ready to meet him down
by the beach. It is a sunny day and I am looking forward to spending
time swimming and having fun. But when I arrive at the beach I see my
husband flirting with a woman with long blonde hair, wearing a black
bathing suit. I try to get his attention but he doesn't notice me and continues to flirt with this woman. I awake feeling sick to my stomach.*

My client was uncomfortable sharing this dream with her husband.
In the past, when she felt suspicious of him, he would gaslight her and
spin the conversation to where she felt foolish for sharing her concerns.
After two more similar dreams and one more counseling session with
me, she finally confronted her husband who once again deflected her
fears. After three months of inner work and trusting her dreams, she
initiated a marital separation which led to an honest discussion with
her husband where he admitted to having a brief affair with an old
flame. At that point, they committed to couples counseling.

Matters of trust cut deep and can cause trauma to the soul, prompting
people to shut down their heart. Marc Ian Barasch writes: "We cannot

have it both ways, say our dreams: it is by love that our lives are woven together, because of love that the delicate strands strum. There are no secrets, dreams tell us, especially from the heart."

Trust continues to be a deep wound for my client and recovering from such secrecy and deception may take a very long time. Yet she remains bravely committed to keeping her heart open, perhaps not as open with her husband, but unlocked to her wiser woman self.

The watery realm of emotional dreams

Emotional dreams differ in that the *feelings* are prominent. Dr. Ernest Hartmann, known for his dream and sleep disorder research, refers to these as "tidal wave dreams." After a disturbing experience, the dreamer often finds himself walking down the beach, when suddenly a tidal wave appears and washes over him but he survives. Or, the dreamer is standing outdoors, when suddenly she sees a large locomotive barreling down the track and it comes close to hitting her. Hartmann found a correlation between our waking life upset and the intensity of emotions during dreamtime.

In my own experience, I have had many dreams where the emotions were very strong and the key to understanding the deeper message. Frankly, I believe that the emotional energy in dreams is downplayed by many experts and takes a back seat to dream images and themes. And too often, a dream is analyzed—*an intellectual process*—leaving the feelings in the dust.

How you *feel* during your dream is invaluable to understanding it. You may write down a dream about walking along a beach, when suddenly you see large waves looming before you, growing in size and intensity, so you move closer to land where it is safer. That's fine and dandy, but what were you *feeling* when you noticed the waves? When you identify the feelings you might notice that you were very scared when you first saw the waves and became really frightened as they grew in size and intensity. Your feelings add layers of dimension and meaning to the dream that point the way to what you are truly experiencing about something in your waking life. Here is an example of a dream a woman once shared:

> *I am a young child, about three or four years old, riding in the backseat of*
> *a car. My father and mother are in the front seat and my grandmother is*
> *sitting next to me in the backseat. My father is driving down a road that*

curves, when suddenly the car goes off the road and we begin to slide down
a large hill. I am looking out the window as we continue to roll down the
side of this hill.

When the dreamer first presented this dream, she was unemotional, detached, and her affect was flat. She stated she felt "fine" about the dream because she awoke before anything "bad" happened. However, as we replayed this dream and delved into her emotional energy field, she remembered feeling "terrified" as the car slid off the road and began rolling down the hill. She also felt very "sad" that her beloved grandmother may get hurt, and "angry" that her father hadn't been more careful and her mother didn't stop him from swerving off the road.

Digging a little deeper, we discovered that the dreamer frequently experienced these same feelings when she was growing up; her father was prone to emotional outbursts, while her mother tended to isolate and shut down her feelings. The dreamer found solace spending time with her grandmother who died when she was young. Reviewing her current life, we connected some essential dots. The dreamer was involved with a man she felt controlled by and she felt he was "driving" her life. She was ready to reclaim her power and independence yet having a difficult time changing some old patterns.

Remaining focused on her feelings in both the dream and waking situation, we did some role playing where I encouraged the dreamer to imagine facing the man and verbally expressing her feelings. After a few practice rounds, using a process called active imagination (discussed in detail in Chapter 6), I invited the dreamer to imagine herself as the strong, wise woman she was becoming, and to see herself sitting next to the younger version of herself in the backseat of the car. Her wise-woman self added the protection and safety her younger self needed while she was growing up, and in her current life with the controlling partner. Eventually, the dreamer felt empowered enough to tell her father he was no longer driving the car and that she was taking the wheel. We concluded our process by the dreamer seeing and feeling herself driving the car comfortably along the curvy road until she reached a safe destination point. In her case, it was a public beach access point that overlooked the Pacific Ocean where she often parked because it made her feel serene and centered.

The most common emotional dream consists of strong feelings that are lasting, and sometimes these dreams are hard to awake from because emotional energy can be dense. Grief, anger, fear are examples of emotional dreams and we have them because we are in need of feeling these feelings but may be unable to during waking life. Here is an example of a client who shared an emotional dream. She was estranged from her sister and though she felt okay while awake, her nighttime dream painted a very different picture:

> I am with my sister, dad, and stepmother in a small town; the buildings are very old and surrounding the town are acres of land and open space. I tell my sister: "Take this in, because in ten years, you won't see this again, anywhere." As I state this, I see rows of houses appearing in the background; soulless, boring construction ... Now I am sitting in a rocking chair and my sister is standing behind me, bent down, with her arms wrapped around mine. She hugs me close and starts rocking me, back and forth. It feels extremely comforting. I feel some tears well up in my eyes and think, "Okay, she's probably had enough," so I begin to move my arms to let go. But my sister feels this and tightens her arms around me even more. I awake and feel very heavy from the grief that arose during my dream. My body feels like it is under water.

The past is alive in the landscape where the dream begins. The dreamer focuses on the acreage that she believes will be developed over time, reflecting her feelings of being boxed in and claustrophobic from the grief that she has not given herself permission to feel. She experiences being rocked and nurtured by her sister and her desire to be comforted and express her grief is so strong it floods her entire body. Two weeks after this dream session, my client shared that this dream led to grief work and that she felt much lighter as a result. As time unfolded, she continued healing through her grief and releasing some old, co-dependent patterns she had with her sister. Eventually she was reconciled with her sister and cultivated a bond that was more authentic.

Put it into practice!

- When writing down your dream, ask yourself: *What did I feel during the dream? Anger, surprise, confusion, sadness, terror, relief, etc.*, then circle those emotions in your dream journal.
- Are these feelings present, lurking underneath the surface during waking life?

- What dream images correspond with your feelings? For example: *When I felt sad, I dreamt I was in a large lake and the water was murky.*
- Pay attention to your feelings during dreamtime and notice if there is a theme that arises. For example, you may discover that you feel angry while dreaming and the color dark red frequently appears, perhaps in the image of dark red car, coat, or hair color. These are clues from the unconscious. You may find it difficult to express your anger in waking life, or are carrying repressed anger that is ready to be expressed in constructive ways.

The illuminating realm of spiritual dreams

Spiritual dreams are unmistakable. This type of dream will leave you feeling inspired, motivated, whole, and at peace. Spiritual dreams create the greatest transformative impact out of all the dreams you will ever have. They stand out and are rarely forgotten. Imbued with distinct characteristics, they leave an indelible mark on your heart and soul that may affect you for a very long time. In fact, it's not uncommon to glean incredible insight from this type of dream, information that will assist you in various areas throughout the rest of your life. Spiritual dreams have the ability to give your life new meaning and offer a higher perspective on life in general. Spiritual dreams are most likely to occur during the following times in your life:

1) Before a significant change
2) Prior to, or as you're experiencing a shift in perception about yourself and your life
3) After a commitment to something meaningful has been expressed and is genuinely being pursued
4) Following a major loss or change
5) When becoming more aware of yourself, your circumstances, your life
6) During emotional and spiritual breakthroughs, such as taking a class, attending therapy, practicing yoga or meditation
7) During a recovery process.

Spiritual dream symbols

How do you know when you're having a spiritual dream? Well, along with becoming aware of the inspired feelings you may experience, certain symbols are likely to appear. These include light, bright colors, candle, clear water (or any body of water that is clear), higher self figures like wizard, angel, fairy, old man; spiritual or religious books, cross, star, sun, moon, lotus, mandala, labyrinth, rainbow, sea, rose, stone, tree, mountain top, music, or any symbol that has spiritual significance to you. Many of the symbols that I have included are considered archetypes since they carry universal meaning.

Your spiritual energy centers

Another way to distinguish a spiritual dream from other dreams is to notice if the dream pertains to one of the spiritual energy centers. These involve both the endocrine system (in Western cultures) and chakras (in Eastern). There are seven energy centers and they are as follows:

Seventh Center: Crown Chakra (Prayer Center), Color: Violet, Planet: Jupiter. Being attuned to our divinity, Nature, and having a sense of oneness with other living beings on the planet dwell within the crown chakra. The energy that aligns with this chakra is a strong sense of "I AM." Imbalances in this energy center are often experienced as feeling spiritually disconnected, loneliness, isolation, difficulty in completing goals, and an overall lack of purpose.

Sixth Center: Third Eye Chakra (Intuition), Color: Indigo, Planet: Mercury. Our ability to use our intuitive and imagination along with our dreams and fantasies reside in this chakra. Light is the element and the affirmation is "I SEE." Blockages or imbalances in this energy center manifest as not trusting what we feel, losing sight of what is important, and becoming stagnant. Physical symptoms can occur such as migraines, sinusitis, and poor vision.

Fifth Center: Throat Chakra (Communication), Color: Blue, Planet: Uranus. Our ability to clearly express ourselves, to giving voice to what matters most, and expressing our creativity are core aspects of this chakra. Sound is the element and the affirmation is "I SPEAK." When we have difficulty setting boundaries, saying "no," and expressing ourselves we can be sure there is some blockage and imbalance in the throat chakra. A client who had been working on speaking her truth to her father shared a dream that illustrates the power of this center:

> *I am in the car with my father, he is driving and I am in the passenger seat. We're going to a relative's house for dinner and he begins lecturing me about*

not spending enough time with my family. I'm afraid of making him angry but I raise my right hand and say, "Stop!" He looks at me with disbelief but I keep on talking. "I've had enough of you trying to control me and I'm not going to put up with it anymore!" My voice escalates and I notice that my father's neck is turning a bluish-red color. I tell my father to stop the car and he does, so I get out and begin walking down a road, back to my home.

Because this woman did not feel comfortable telling her father how she felt when she was awake, her true feelings emerged during the safety of dreamtime. This particular dream was grist for her soul's mill because it empowered my client to speak truthfully to her father over a period of time. A year after having the dream, she reported that her relationship with her father had improved, not because it was any easier to be around him, but because she felt more authentic.

Fourth Center: Heart Chakra (Giving and Receiving Love), Color: Green, Planet: Venus. Our ability to express compassion, empathy, joy, and love toward ourselves and others resides within this chakra. Air is the element and the affirmation is "I LOVE." Holding onto resentments, fear of betrayal, anger, bitterness, and feeling guarded reflect imbalances within this chakra.

Third Center: Solar Plexus Chakra (Personal Power, Sense of Self), Color: Yellow, Planet: Mars. This chakra embodies personal power, choices, and self-motivation. Fire is the element and this chakra resonates to "I CAN." Imbalances in the third chakra may cause us to suffer from low self-esteem, difficulty in making decisions, and channeling our anger in a destructive manner. Here is an example of a dream I once had involving my sense of self as a writer:

I am part of a technical and science expo and James Hillman calls me into his office. "You can pick anything that I've created and develop it." It's a very favorable offer and I feel excited about delving into his theory on archetypal psychology and dream work.

Now I am in a huge bed with white sheets and Kelsey Grammer joins me. In a businesslike tone he says, "I want my biography written and I think you might be the person to write it. Do you know much about my character on the show Frasier?" I think, "Oh my god, do you have any idea how well I know your character? He shows me a large piece of glossy paper decorated with different colorful ink patterns and I realize he's offering me the position to write Frasier's biography.

I am now in a room with a former boss who acknowledges my bio-graphical assignment and informs me I can work on it one hour a day. I think, "Are you kidding, I will devote a lot more time to it than that." Then a few female coworkers appear and challenge me, "You can't write it while you're working!" I reply, "Yes, I can and it will generate $50,000." I instantly regret stating that amount because I think it's too low.

This dream has numerous elements involving opportunity, potential, creativity, abundance, and self-worth. More specifically, it reveals how the animus figures (Hillman, Grammer, former male boss) amplify my worth, while the female shadow (negative coworkers) attempt to limit my opportunities. This has been an ongoing theme throughout my life and stems from some early childhood experiences with an older sibling who, when feeling threatened by me, would attempt to sabotage my success. As much as I worshipped her as a child, it took years of inner work before I felt free to follow my own path and give myself permission to succeed as an adult.

Second Center: Sacral Chakra, Lower Abdomen Chakra (Relationship with Others), Color: Orange, Planet: Neptune. This chakra resides in the pelvic region and reflects sexuality, pleasure, procreativity. Water is the element and the affirmation is "I CREATE." This chakra supports us accessing and identifying our feelings and where we desire to channel our energy and attention. Signs of being imbalanced with this chakra might appear as feeling jealous, possessive, controlling, or having issues with our sexuality, for example, low libido, sexual dysfunction, etc.

First Center: Root Chakra (Tribal Belonging), Color: Red, Planet: Saturn. This chakra sits at the base of the spine and symbolizes survival and belonging. Earth is the element and this chakra allows us to feel grounded and secure. "I BELONG" and "I MATTER" are how this chakra is best expressed. Issues involving feeling unwanted, not centered, and insecure reveal an imbalance with the first chakra.

Your physical body provides a means of communication for your soul. At the same time, your spiritual body allows you to experience higher levels of consciousness and the capacity to attain mastery over the physical realm. The connecting point for these two bodies is in the spiritual centers. Through meditation, you can learn to balance the energy that flows between these centers. Dreams can show you the different levels of awareness through symbols and themes. For example, a dream of a wise old man and the number seven may be telling you that you are dreaming at the seventh level of awareness, the crown chakra. Or, dreaming of the color yellow and of some type of fire may suggest that there is some attunement needed in your third spiritual center. Notice any chakra elements that surface during dreamtime, such as water or light. These can help you identify what energy center your dream is communicating to you and whether or not there is an imbalance.

Spiritual dreams appear the least of any dream type, so when you have one, pay particular attention to it. Allow yourself to sink into the feelings of well-being as long as possible. They tend to happen when you are going through some form of transformation. Reading inspiring spiritual material before falling asleep, meditating, praying, and setting your intentions will enhance your ability to experience these types of dreams. During waking life, letting go of past resentments, opening your heart, practicing gratitude, and self-forgiveness can also inspire spiritual dreams.

Put it into practice!

Check your dream journal and choose a dream that "calls" to you. Take a few moments to answer the questions below.

- Are there any spiritual dream symbols?
- Do any colors stand out?
- What emotions were present?
- Which energy center is showing up?
- Do you see any imbalances that the dream is pointing to?
- Can you see how your dream is providing numerous clues, enhancing your awareness, and supporting you in moving forward purposefully with love, strength, and grace?

CHAPTER FOUR

Who are these cast of characters?

Everything that irritates us about others can lead us to an understanding of ourselves.

—Carl Jung

Have you ever wondered why an ex-partner, Uncle John, Cousin Zack, or your neighbor appear in your dream? What about complete strangers showing up? Perhaps you haven't even seen some of the people starring in your dream for a long time. Furthermore, maybe you don't even *like* some of these characters. Yet they show up causing you to ask yourself, "Why them? Why now? What do they have to do with me?"

Perhaps one of our greatest challenges—and rewards—when working with dreams is understanding our dream characters. In Chapter 3, the third dream key discussed how every dream character is an aspect of us, the dreamer. In this section, we are going to dive deeper into why certain people are playing the lead in your dreams. We will also examine the three archetypes which Carl Jung calls the shadow, anima, and animus. These three prototypes parade through dreamtime on numerous occasions, in myriad forms. They possess a wealth of information about what is *really* going on inside of us, yet are frequently unrecognized and misunderstood. As we give these characters attention and attempt to truly understand them, we discover how they possess the ability to lead us toward wholeness, individuation, and self-realization unlike anything else.

"Dreams show us," Robert Johnson states, "in symbolic form, all the different personalities that interact within us and make up our total self." Since dreams emerge from the unconscious, they support us in achieving individuation—the process of moving toward the realization of our complete and whole inner self. From this perspective, dreams play an essential role in the individuation process because they reveal the different aspects, or personalities of ourselves which appear as dream figures.

Think about it: Don't you behave differently when you are around your closest friend versus your colleague, boss, spouse, or neighbor? We tend to believe we are one person with one personality, but if we stop and notice, we discover that we have myriad people living inside us, sometimes tugging us in different directions. What in our interior realm causes us to feel split or conflicted by these different persons? I possess a strong spiritual side but have an equally powerful opinionated, analytical, sexual, and renegade side. Dream figures provide a discovery process for unearthing these uniquely diverse facets, but only when I am open to accepting them as parts of the whole "me." So it is vital to tend gently to dream figures and not judge them harshly, even the very frightening ones. Every dream matters as does every dream character. The more disturbing a dream character is, the more we should want to employ *curiosity*.

For example, a woman with long, red hair appears during your dream and you are upset with her for being so critical of you. You get into an argument with her and attempt to explain your actions, yet she reacts indifferently and minimizes your feelings. You awake feeling confused, thinking, "I don't recognize this woman and I'm not anything like her, she's negative and mean."

However, this dream figure possesses a wealth of information. She may be reflecting back to you the aspect of yourself that feels angry toward someone and needs to express it. Or, perhaps you have been critical toward yourself and it's preventing you from moving forward. She may seem like a stranger since you do not recognize her in the dream or waking life, but she is a part of you that you do not yet recognize within yourself. Unfamiliar individuals and groups of people embody traits of you that psyche is trying to bring to consciousness to support you in integrating these aspects, leading you toward greater psychological wholeness.

But what if you recognize the character starring in your dream? Familiar faces often represent aspects you recognize, but do not *identify* with ... yet. As I mentioned, soul casts characters in your dreams which reflect aspects of you, so when your friend, Brianna, appears in last night's dream, the first key is to get in touch with your perception of her. If you were sharing your dream with me, I would ask the following probes:

1) How would you describe Brianna?
2) What is your relationship with Brianna like right now?
3) When you think about Brianna, how do you feel?
4) If a stranger were asking you about Brianna, what top five adjectives would you use to explain your observations of Brianna?

The second step is to consider which one or more traits you perceive Brianna possesses is showing up in your behavior. If you see Brianna in a negative fashion, then this stage of the process can be very difficult. Dream figures may appear as frightening, vindictive, cruel, hateful, domineering, wimpy, prejudiced, passive-aggressive, punishing, and even murderous. These qualities reside within all of us even though we may not act them out or want to believe we have them, so it's important we practice as little judgment as possible when tending to our dream figures.

When dream characters are playing themselves

Sometimes, a dream figure appears that you recognize because of your relationship with him or her. Perhaps you are actively involved in a relationship with this person and your dream is revealing some issue(s) that need to be addressed. In this case, such characters appearing are playing themselves and the dream is a *relationship* dream. Therefore, in this situation, we would notice our current connection with this dream figure, paying particular attention to our feelings, communication, and reactions during the dream.

For example, Cousin Luke appears in your dream and in waking life, you have regular contact with him. So is Cousin Luke appearing as himself, or, is he mirroring aspects of you? One rule of thumb is to observe your relationship and notice if there are concerns you have about your connection with Luke. For example, sometimes my husband appears as my masculine aspect, while other times he shows up as himself. I can usually delineate between the two when I tap into our current connection and notice if there is an important issue or concern I am experiencing. Again, the unconscious brings dream figures to help us expand our awareness about ourselves and our relationships, and are an amazing tool for addressing issues and healing them.

Put it into practice!

Let's examine a dream where a dream figure is prominent.

- Do you know this person, or is he/she a stranger?
- How do you feel about this person?
- If you recognize this person, what is your relationship with this person? Do you have current contact with this person?
- When you think of this person, what is your perception of him/her? (Often, when I'm counseling someone with his/her dreams, I'll ask this question only to hear the person respond, "I don't know." This is a typical response in the beginning. Practice is necessary to be able to tap into your perception of another person. But with focus and consistency, you'll know immediately what someone represents to you when she or he appears.)

Begin making a list of dream figures and following the above process. With practice, you will be able to more quickly identify the qualities which the dream figure represents to you, increasing your self-awareness on myriad levels.

CHAPTER FIVE

The hidden power of the anima, animus, and shadow

Since he is animus, his seeking has also to do with finding the fully initiated feminine in the psyche and keeping that as the main goal, regardless of whatever else crosses his path ... this animus is doing the real work in preparation for showing and acting the true soul-Self of the newly initiated woman in day-to-day life.

—Clarissa Pinkola Estés

Jung discovered that within us reside both feminine and masculine qualities and psyche is continually seeking to synthesize the two. Whether or not we are a man or a woman, our androgynous self is seeking to integrate the feminine with the masculine into the archetype of the *divine marriage*. Female dream characters represent the feminine qualities: nurturing, sensitive, emotional, intuitive, gentle, receptive, and caring. Male dream characters reveal our masculine aspects: doing, action, intellect, assertive, down-to-earth, and willpower. Therefore, when a woman appears in your dreams, notice the feminine qualities she embodies. Is she passive, bold, fearful, nurturing, outspoken, or timid? When we are aligned with the feminine, or *feeling-function*, we are able to identify and express our feelings, practice self-love and compassion for others, listen deeply to what others are saying, seek understanding, and trust our intuition. When a man shows up in your dream, observe his behavior and notice how you would describe him. Is he determined, bossy, sensual, heroic, tyrannical, controlling, or creative?

Jung referred to the archetypal feminine presence in a man's dream as the *anima*, and the archetypal masculine presence in a woman's dream as the *animus*. In Latin, the words *anima* and *animus* mean *soul*. Becoming aware of these archetypal images is essential in our emotional, intellectual, and psychological development.

I have been working with the animus for the past twenty years. He frequently appears in my dreams when I desire to move forward with an idea, project, or task and need to harness the "doing" aspect that enables me to give birth to an idea and bring into reality. He has also emerged when I was ready to work through my "wounded male" aspect, the masculine qualities that I repressed from patriarchal childhood and cultural programming. In my twenties, men would materialize as frightening, dangerous shadow figures who pursued me. As I began working with these images, they begin to shift. In my thirties, an ex-partner surfaced as distant and aloof, but not dangerous, so my fear diminished. In my forties, after more years of tending to these important dream figures, the ex-partner appeared friendly, caring, and supportive. As the years continue to unfold, I found myself in loving embraces with this dream figure and often we got married. I always awake from these dreams feeling extremely happy and never want them to end. Animus shifted from a frightening male to a loving ex-partner who symbolized my inner lover.

Dreaming Eros: the god of inner love

Eros often manifests in dreamtime as the lover archetype. When Eros appears all our senses are aroused. We are filled with the same aliveness that we feel in the beginning of an intimate relationship; colors appear brighter, aromas smell intoxicating, and every day oozes with the nectar of life. In dreamtime, Eros gives us vital life force energy. In our relationships, Eros provides the embers which feed our connection; without it, we feel barren, disconnected, and wondering, "Where did the passion go?" I've counseled numerous couples who still love one another but are deeply missing the beginning arc of passion that brought them together.

Sometimes this leads to projecting our inner Eros onto a human being which leads to problems. "If we mistake a human lover for our Inner Lover," writes Stephen Aizenstat, "we can experience even the slightest of criticisms as rejection by Eros."

There was a time when I experienced this exact phenomenon. I met someone when I was vulnerable and feeling burned out from all my responsibilities. Work consumed my life and my role necessitated the masculine qualities of planning, delegating, and leading. I felt disconnected from my feminine self, estranged from my soul. Not surprisingly, the man I attracted, and was attracted to, revered what he perceived to be the ultimate woman: beautiful, wise, supportive, passive. I fell down the rabbit hole of infatuation, abandoned my masculine aspect, and let him lead the way. It felt exhilarating, refreshing, and passion ensued.

In archetypal alchemy, the alchemical king and queen symbolize *sol* (solar/rational, masculine mind) and *luna* (lunar/heart, feminine energy). Leading Jungian analyst, Edward Edinger, explains that during our search for Eros we are seeking the alchemical marriage of these two aspects. The human man was pure "sol" energy: energetic, restless, and full of vigor. I, on the other hand, with my passion for the night sky, full moon, and dreams, brought "luna's" qualities into the alchemical cauldron. Edinger discusses how these energies, when transformed, become the lovers, who were once opposites and are now connected into inseparable wholeness. However, I was stuck in the infatuation phase and nothing had transformed, or was about to transform, at this stage of the game.

Interestingly, during this time, the ongoing stream of animus dreams I had been having ceased completely. It wasn't until a year later after we stopped seeing each other that they gradually resumed, and when they did, my animus was distant, resentful, and bitter. I couldn't help but wonder, "What happened? Why did the remarkably loving dreams that brought me so much happiness end?"

Erroneously, I had projected my Eros/inner lover fantasies onto the waking life man. Getting swept away by the fervidness of romance, I unconsciously suppressed my authentic self: I changed the way I dressed, the way I behaved, the way I thought about certain issues in order to fulfill his desires. It's no big surprise that I lost myself. Conversely, his ego projected his highest ideals onto me. Like many middle-aged men, he was ready to deepen his connection with his inner self and longed for spiritual sustenance. My spirituality—a significant part of my life—was what his soul desired, and eventually he began exploring the realm of his own spiritual nature.

Thanatos: a misunderstood cry for differentiation

Eros has its shadow side: Thanatos. Most of us are familiar with the magnetic pull of Eros and the passion we feel when we fall in love. But Thanatos is equally as powerful and important but often overlooked. Thanatos is the god of death in Greek mythology, the god of sleep. If we are in a long-term relationship, we know how important it becomes to create space for ourselves as the relationship evolves. It's a healthy way of differentiating from a partner. This means setting boundaries, spending time apart to nurture our soul, delving into creative projects or activities that fulfill us, and allowing our partner the same freedoms. When we don't recognize the need to differentiate, or believe there is something "wrong" with the relationship, we are denying the qualities of Thanatos.

While counseling clients I have witnessed the times when Thanatos has reared its head. And frequently, couples believe that because they want more space or time apart from their partner, it must mean one, or both of them, want out. Eros appears to have died and passion has been replaced with the partner's flaws. Instead of wanting to be with them, we desire more and more time away and alone.

If left unrecognized, this is when the relationship becomes confusing, the couple experiences disillusionment, and/or a breakdown or uncoupling begins.

Carl G. Jung believed that how we behave stems from the different way we use our mental capacities. From this concept, Katharine Cook Briggs and her daughter Isabel Briggs Myers created the Myers-Briggs Type Indicator. This instrument has been used for many years and helps people clarify their basic personality type. The "intuitive-feeling" person relates deeply to the Romeo and Juliet archetype and the idea of falling madly, deeply in love with his or her soul mate. These personality types are particularly sensitive to the power of Eros and crazily happy when experiencing the beginning throes of a relationship. However, when Thanatos begins to creep in, this personality type often experiences distress. *Where did my beloved go?!* Desiring time apart may feel so contrary to earlier days that the relationship must be doomed.

Yet, Eros is impossible to experience without Thanatos. Thanatos represents a time in the relationship to honor the distancing, confusion, and estrangements as a meaningful progression toward expanding the relationship. It allows Eros to become renewed and remain alive. Therefore, this is a crucial time to individually expand within the relationship, as well as stretch the comfort zone of the relationship itself. This critical juncture can lead to death of the relationship *or* to two people learning to differentiate which can lead to individuation. Strong communication and creative ways to support the changes are required. Patience and trust that growth is occurring are also helpful.

How does Thanatos appear in dreams?

During dreamtime, Thanatos may appear in myriad ways. For example, a woman may have animus dreams where she is trying to pull away or escape from him. Rather than trying to connect with him as in dreams of Eros, she wants to replace him in the driver's seat. She may dream of living alone or wanting to kill her animus. More literal dreams may appear where she is leaving her partner or expressing anger toward him in a series of dreams. During waking time, she may fantasize of leaving the relationship, moving away, opening herself to meeting someone new, and so forth. As always, *feelings* are key. Irritation, anger, resentment, confusion, fear—these emotions are pointing the way to what psyche and soul are trying to communicate. Her anger is a symptom of a deeper issue; if she is denying Thanatos and the need for differentiation, her resentment will grow either toward her partner or herself depending upon her ability to access her feelings and express them. Following is an example of Thanatos appearing during dreamtime:

> I am with an attractive woman and we are in a large outdoor park, like Yellowstone, or a similar environment. We are hiking and it is a gray day and cold. She is standing at the edge of a cliff looking down at the ravine below. I am behind her and have the urge to push her off the cliff. It's something I have been considering for a while. As I approach her someone yells from behind me and stops me. I awake feeling ashamed and confused.

In waking life, having been married for eighteen years to the love of his life, this dreamer was struggling. He had cultivated a successful career and desired more time on his own to express his creative side through photography, writing poetry, and painting. However, he and his wife were used to spending most of their time together when they were not working. He was worried she would feel neglected if he carved out time for himself, especially because he worked so many hours. So he kept his feelings to himself and his resentment grew. Until they came to counseling, he didn't know his wife was experiencing similar feelings. Although her desire for time alone was not as strong as his, she had been fantasizing about traveling to new places, *without him*. She felt telling him about her needs would cause him to feel insecure or threaten the relationship so she said nothing.

In reality, this couple desired something that was not only healthy but would evolve their relationship. By giving himself permission to create, the man would feed his soul and develop more of his feeling function thereby enhancing his *anima* qualities. Likewise, the woman allowing herself to travel to new places—without her husband—would help her strengthen her *animus* aspects: independence, inner strength, courage, action.

Thanatos does not mean a relationship is dying, quite the opposite. It is a primary opportunity for the soul to be heard and to communicate one's needs in an honest, loving, respectful manner, and then to make the necessary changes to accommodate each other's requests.

The strength of the anima and animus reflects the inner marriage, or *hieros gamos*, the stabilizing of masculine and feminine aspects, a significant part of our journey toward individuation. This leads us to the following section in which we will explore the profound meaning of the anima and animus.

The anima and animus: divine integration

A man who is not in touch with his feeling-function, meaning he has difficulty identifying and expressing his feelings, may project his anima onto his female partner, expecting her to carry the emotional pressure of the relationship. For example, a husband might feel deep grief over the loss of a parent, yet, because he is unable to feel his pain, he may unconsciously provoke his wife until *she* becomes emotionally upset. In this case, he has projected his repressed anima onto *her*, making her responsible for *his* feelings.

Examining where there is a distinct split between our masculine and feminine selves, Anne Baring, coauthor of *The Divine Feminine: Exploring the Feminine Face of God Throughout the World* once wrote, the masculine aspect "becomes pathologically exaggerated, inflated; the feminine pathologically diminished, inarticulate, ineffective." Like my Eros adventure with my inner lover and human male, I was out of alignment with my feminine and masculine aspects. Baring discusses this phenomenon in the fairytale *Sleeping Beauty*: "Sleeping Beauty symbolizes the lunar principle of soul, the feeling values (Eros) and in essence, this fairy-tale is about the alchemical marriage of the sun and the moon. Thus, when the prince (solar/rational mind) connects with Sleeping Beauty (lunar/heart energy), she and her entire sleeping court awaken."

Tending to the anima and animus moves us toward individuation. Jungian analyst, Marion Woodman, speaks to the enormous importance of the animus when she writes, "So long as we fail to do the hard work of bringing our own masculine and feminine sides to consciousness, we fall back upon those ancient parental figures who have long since hardened into the established forms which reinforce a patriarchal order." These two aspects reside within everyone and our dreams reveal where we are out of balance with one or both aspects. They contain an intelligence which supports us in connecting with both aspects so we can attain integration, balance, harmony, and wholeness. Having balance between your feminine and masculine selves is essential to your emotional, intellectual, and spiritual well-being and your dreams are a powerful vehicle for achieving balance between both of these energies.

Facing our shadow figures

The shadow material is the fire of the unconscious. That is, it can be a powerful force for creation or destruction. Handled properly, it can heal us of our deepest psychological difficulties. Its energy becomes life affirming and enhancing rather than crippling and depleting.

—Stephen Aizenstat

Dreams lead us into the vivid realm of the unconscious, an incredible force of power in our human experience revealing a full spectrum of conflicts—inner and outer. These clashes entail our desires, ethics, beliefs, fears, devotions, and exist whether we acknowledge them or not. Most of us are blinded by our judgments, perceptions, and ego-based beliefs that prevent us from seeing our inner skirmishes. We cling to superficial values and behaviors repressing the voice of the unconscious, trying desperately to look anywhere but inward. Yet as the Taoist master Lao Tzu wisely questioned, *how far is the distance between what we consider good and evil?* When we are ready, our nightly dreams provide the fertile soil for witnessing the conflicts awaiting our recognition, and eventually our acceptance which is when the *real* awakening begins. Dreams possess the alchemy to synthesize the opposites, to bridge the gap between good and evil, guiding us toward wholeness.

Carl Jung viewed the shadow as something "a person has no wish to be." He also recognized that it is an essential aspect of the individuation process and of becoming more whole and authentic. The shadow points the way to our inner struggles and quite often appears as the same gender as the dreamer. It possesses traits within us that we dislike, or the qualities that we have not yet learned to assimilate or develop. Since we cannot stand to see these part of ourselves, they get condemned to the "basement" and sit in our unconscious until we are willing to bring them into the light and see them clearly. Ram Dass once taught, "The shadow is the greatest teacher for how to come to the light."

For example, in 1994, I attended a nine-day program focused on releasing and healing the negative traits we "adopt" from our parents, or caregivers. There were twenty-four participants and professionally trained therapists on hand. During the first part of the intensive we centered on "mother's day," a process for identifying and discharging the most undesirable aspects of our mothers, then switched our focus toward our fathers. Because my mother was mentally and physically challenged most of my life, I carried a plethora of unresolved baggage. Not only had I lost her emotionally when I was very young to illness and addiction, I lost her physically when I was twenty-six, and the accumulation of loss created a deep wound filled with rage, pain, and immense grief. After a significant amount of releasing and being guided through a process of compassionate forgiveness, I left the program feeling lighter than I had ever felt before and was happy to return home and share my buoyancy and joy with my husband and daughter. However, a few nights after returning home, I had the following dream:

> *My mother is standing in front of me and I cannot see her clearly, only the shadowy outline of her body but I can hear her very well. Her tone is reprimanding: "You think you have gotten rid of me but you haven't. I'm still here and all of those negative patterns you spent so much time on are still here as well. So stop acting superior and thinking you have eliminated me."*

I awoke feeling disturbed and very confused. I wondered, "Was my mother trying to communicate with me from the other side? Why was she angry? I thought she would be happy for me lightening my load and feeling forgiveness toward her as a result of the process!"

It wasn't until nineteen years later that I more fully understood the full effect of this dream. After more years of studying dreams and completing three years of coursework in a depth psychological graduate program entailing a good deal of work on *shadow*, I finally realized that my attempt to eliminate "negative" aspects of myself does not work! The shadow aspects of my mother within me called for awareness, acceptance, and *integration*, not elimination. Coming to terms with what we perceive as negative gently moves us closer to understanding and accepting these parts of us we dislike. Self-love takes us to the next step: transformation and integration. We can channel our attention on to the "positive" all we want, but until we take a long look at the thoughts, feelings, and behaviors we abhor and begin to understand their significance in our lives, we remain fragmented and dissociated. "For what is life," Lynne Namka penned, "but alternate times of life and shadow? When we work out the shadow part in our self, the times of the shadow are not so dark." Opening an empathic window to these vital pieces of ourselves who have been hiding in the shadow for a very long time, is a necessary step toward becoming authentically whole.

The light side of the shadow

Not every aspect of shadow is "negative." Like everything else in life, it has its light side and is a natural part of the personality. However, like the darker shadow traits, these positive facets are also unconscious and difficult to detect. We may not have assimilated and developed them or pushed them down for various reasons. One might wonder, "Why would we not want to see the positive aspects of ourselves?" Recognizing our strengths, talents, and gifts entails taking responsibility for what we know. Once you know that you have a hidden talent, for example, the gift of writing, then *not* expressing this aptitude in some way, shape, or form will cause pain for your soul. Or, perhaps you enjoyed writing poetry when you were younger but never felt encouraged or supported. So over the years you squelched this forte and now it is buried and long forgotten.

The light side of the shadow can appear in dreams (and waking life) in interesting ways. Think about someone you deeply admire because of a talent or gift they possess. Who is this person and what quality do they have that you hold in high esteem? Their spiritual depth, authenticity, soulfulness, inner peace, confidence, grace, connection with others? Do you believe it is something that they are blessed with but you may never experience? When we deeply admire a quality in someone but secretly believe we are not capable of cultivating it ourselves, it can lead to projecting the light side of the shadow onto others. We tend to do this with role models and leaders who inspire us, thinking they have something special that we do not have, which leads to projecting unconscious aspects of ourselves onto them and elevating them. This halo effect is dangerous for a couple of reasons:

1) Inevitably they will make a mistake, trip up and fall, which can trigger disappointment, disillusionment, and skepticism.
2) We inhibit ourselves from developing the attribute we see in them which stunts our emotional, intellectual, and psychological growth.

For example, a client who was writing a memoir shared the following dream:

> I am riding in a car with a beautiful African American woman and she is driving. I think I am naked or at least partially nude. She begins singing and her voice sounds amazing. Her right arm is lightly touching my left elbow and I am so happy to be riding in the car with her. I comment on how beautifully she sings and she states anyone can sing if they truly want to. I protest saying I have tried singing but have never been able to sing very well. She encourages me to start singing while we're traveling in the car and I feel anxious about singing in front of her.

When this dream appeared, the dreamer was struggling to finish her book. She had a deadline for completing her memoir but found herself sabotaging her progress. Together, we began working with her dreams to uncover the fears and conflicts inhibiting her ability to write. Within a couple of weeks, the above dream surfaced and called to her in an unforgettable way. As we tended to this dream, the dreamer began to see that she was more than capable of expressing her voice and allowing her words to "sing" through the pages. However, in order to claim this talent, she was forced to look at her resistance toward stepping into her core power and as a successful writer. She discovered that she had been playing small and carrying a pint-sized image of herself, rather than a gifted communicator who shared authentically from her heart. Shattering her former self-image and taking responsibility for liberating herself from her old self-perception was needed, and it was her night-time dreams that revealed this truth.

As she became more open toward facing her shadow material, she began dreaming of women who wished to support her in moving forward, as we see in the above dream. The lovely African American woman with the beautiful voice was the light side of the dreamer's shadow, offering to help the dreamer in her writing adventure. If the dreamer had *not* been open to shadow and attempted to repress it, the woman with the amazing voice may not have surfaced as a beautiful dream image, but a frightening hag or enemy. Likewise, male dreamers may experience the light-shadow figure as a kind brother, old friend, or wise teacher who encourages and inspires.

Shadow energy is fierce and the most sizzling aspect of the unconscious; its material must be handled mindfully. As we assimilate the shadow, blame, resentments, and envy give way to personal accountability, paving the way for deciphering what belongs to whom. Through this process we no longer need to see the world as "us versus other" and reduce the tendency to project. In doing so, we open an empathic window that honors all of ourselves and we are free to experience radical self-forgiveness and self-acceptance.

Put it into practice!

How do we gently access our shadow? Like all inner work it requires bringing the unconscious into consciousness. Here are some ideas to achieve connection with your shadow-self:

- Work with your dreams, they are teeming with figures and images pointing the way to your shadow, both the "dark" and "light" sides.
- Pay attention to those "Freudian slips"! Those words and phrases that seem to tumble off your tongue really do matter.
- Notice your body language. Research reveals 93% of what is communicated is done through the body and matters much more than the words we speak.

- Remain aware of your reactions. The more strongly we respond to something or someone, the more likely we are to project unconscious thoughts, feelings, and perceptions about ourselves onto them that we do not wish to see.
- Blame! Like our reactions, blaming others for what bothers us is a good indication that there is something shadowy lurking inside the interior of our mind.
- Hidden thoughts, motives, and actions. We tend to hide that which we are uncomfortable exhibiting about ourselves. Secrecy, lying to ourselves and others ... these are ways we protect the aspects of ourselves that wish to remain in the dark.

CHAPTER SIX

Dream images: metaphors
of transformation

> *At a certain point in our work with dreams, the images will come and
> touch us directly ... when living images present themselves in such
> a strong way, it is as if life itself is pouring out through them. They
> are like portals to the source of life, connecting us to the process of
> creation ... when we experience images in this way, we feel a sense of
> love and caring.*
>
> —Stephen Aizenstat

How meaningful are your nighttime dream images?

Every day we are hit with thousands of images from today's technological culture; one picture after another is thrust in our faces, often leaving us feeling sterile, barren, and overwhelmed. But a picture is not the same thing as a dream image, nor are our daylight depictions similar to our nocturnal visions. Our dream images are late-night phantasms of the soul. Sourcing midnight metaphors, psyche weaves a tapestry of mystery and wisdom that transports us to the unknown. It pushes us to our edge. What was the last dream image that surprised, confused, or possibly disturbed you? Did you attend to the image or did you dismiss it?

When we embody our nighttime dream images we breathe life into them and rouse them from our slumbering mental chambers. Engaging the dream image opens the pathway to its existence. You discover *why* it is choosing to star in *your* nighttime theater. In fact, activating and animating our most disturbing dream images can unleash their greatest potential. Dream images are alive and reside deep within us.

Dutch Jungian analyst, Robert Bosnak reminds us, "One cannot remove an organ from a human being without altering the entire body, and the same is true of a dream image." Every symbol in your dreams has significant meaning to you, the dreamer, and all objects, persons, sounds, words, landscapes, and colors are unique images that deserve to be seen in their own distinct way. Every dream image has its own soul spark since they are the language of the psyche. The word *psyche* is derived from the Greek word *soul* and psyche, or soul, is expressed through *soma*, or body. "Why," Woodman once wrote, "is the image in the dream a healer? Why is the image in your dream a gift from God? The reason is this: The image works on your imagination, it works on your emotional body, it works on your thinking, and on your intellect. So for a moment, your intellect, emotion and imagination are one. You are whole. The image clicks and that instant your whole being says 'Yes!'"

The soul of an image

All dream images—pleasant and disturbing—are gifts psyche offers us which may be received with repugnance or gratitude. The fact that we are stirred by an image invites a deeper meaning. In *The Dream and the Underworld*, Hillman implies that dreams place us *inside the images*, rather than images inside of us. Hillman teaches that images are whole, complete, and embodied: "Meet the images as *soul*," and pay close attention to your dream images, particularly those that are most disturbing. My experience has been that the more upsetting the dream image, the more important it is to work with.

I once heard renowned storyteller Michael Meade share an ancient African story that entailed an unforgettable image of a face: One side was gold and the other side was rotting flesh, infested with maggots. The image of flesh-eating maggots most likely triggers some form of repugnance and if they appeared in your dream tonight, you might feel disgusted, or at the very least, too embarrassed to share this dream. However, if you are willing to look a little more closely at this image, you might discover that maggots are appearing for an important reason. The tale of the maggot/gold face reveals how the golden aspect (light) could only be seen by allowing the maggots to devour the rotting flesh (dark). They served an essential function of removing the dark overlay that was blocking the gold plate. The metaphor is that in order to see our own light, we must embrace our shadow. The inner healers, symbolized by the maggots, have the capacity to clean up our unconscious inner conflicts and issues. The very dream image that disturbs you may be showing you where the "gold" is if you approach it with curiosity and patience.

Befriending the image with association

Our dreams recover what the world forgets … The dream animal shows us that the imagination has jaws and paws, that it can wake us in the night with panic and terror or move us to tears … and see their living forms so that we respond to them with the gift of intelligence.

—James Hillman

Let's take a deeper look at the power of dream images. The snake in dreamtime is a perfect example because it is powerful and frequently misunderstood. In his book *Dream Animals*, Hillman explains: "… a black snake comes in a dream, a great big black snake, and you can spend a whole hour of therapy with this snake, talking about the devouring mother, talking about anxiety, about repressed sexuality … But what remains after all the symbolic understanding is what that snake is doing, this crawling huge snake that's sliding into your life."

As I mentioned in Chapter 1, snakes have always terrified me. When I began having a series of snake dreams in 2013, they rocked both my dream and waking world until 2016. Snakes of all colors, shapes, and sizes slithered into my dreams and frightened me for the first year. It wasn't until I began experiencing the amazing intelligence of these living images that I shifted from terror to understanding, and then could see the gift these insightful reptiles brought to my life. One of my dream mentors, Dr. Stephen Aizenstat, was instrumental in helping me tend to these confusing and scary snake images. Using his process of "dream tending," I began asking the snake image: "*Who is visiting now?*" This charged question implies a familiarity with the dream image, as though it has appeared many times, dressed in different forms but always with a similar message: Something very important is about to happen, or is happening so, *WAKE UP!*

I also used the process of *association* to experience a deeper meaning of the nightmarish snake images. Association is a no-nonsense, straightforward approach and can be done in very little time. When I first listed my associations of snake, I wrote: slither, slippery, sneaky, constricting, squeezing, poisonous, temptation, flirting, sexual play, seduction, manipulation, power, control, fear, father's belt, physical punishment, men, unsafe. The next round my associations went deeper and I noted: frightened, wound, intimacy, distance, guarded, protective, healing, trauma. *The key is to keep going back to the original dream image and writing down your associations without pausing.* Once you begin thinking about it, you've shifted from psyche to intellect and will lose the deeper meaning. Also, you might become inspired by associations that arise and begin associating *those* images, but don't go there, doing so will cause you to lose sight of the original dream image. Start with one dream image and stick with it until an "aha" moment happens or you feel an inner click. Some associations will have an emotional charge to them and that's where you want to focus.

For example, I continued to work through my associations until some pieces of my dream image puzzle fell into place. Since the snake dreams were frightening and nightmarish, I knew I had to face this image. Nightmares occur when we resist seeing something important and their scary presence commands our attention. Associating with snake helped me understand why snake was showing up and what it was trying to communicate. The longer I worked with association, the less frightening this image became and the more it transformed. In a series of dreams, snake transmuted itself from circling my shoulders for hours leaving me in a trance-like state (dream #1), to sliding up next to me and lying still as I rested my hand against its head (dream #2), to a cluster of water moccasins living under black, jagged rocks (dream #3), to a black snake with a long red tongue that jabbed my lower back (dream #4), to a very large black snake with large dragon-like teeth (dream #5), to a shape-shifter in the following dream:

> *I'm outdoors in a large open space and several feet in front of me is a long, green snake with black stripes. The snake has been living underneath some dense foliage, thick ivy. It has been living under there for a long time but now it's out in the sunlight. I see it has black narrow eyes and then I notice*

two more round black "eyes" above the regular eyes, sitting on either side of its head. Looking more closely, I can see that they react to the light, like sensors and then it gives a very loud rattle.

Next, I see something move around the top of the snake's head and a baby snake with tiny legs unhooks itself and crawls down its face. The baby scoots away and then a very bizarre thing happens: The snake completely transforms itself by pulling its skin forward until it covers its eyes and face. It now looks like a beautiful, large, green succulent that curves downward. I am fascinated and realize I no longer need to fear snakes.

This dream is filled with a wealth of images: large open space, green snake with black stripes, thick ivy, eyes that are sensors, the sound of the rattle, the lizard-like baby snake with legs, transformation from snake into a large succulent. Here is an example of my associations:

- Open space: nature, place I go for reflecting, healing, feeling open-minded, getting grounded, peaceful, favorite place to be
- Green snake: rattlesnake, poisonous, green is a "healing" color, primitive, reptilian, shape-shifter, kundalini energy, sheds its skin
- Thick ivy: I love ivy, dense cover, easy to maintain, grows in my yard, resilient, protective
- Eyes that are sensors: insight, sensitive to light, awareness, vision
- Rattle: Primal, rhythm, Native American, instrument, warning, ancient, felt it in my body
- Baby snake with legs: birth, new beginnings, circle of life, lizard-like
- Transformation into succulent: change, healing, shape-shifter, awakening, verdant, alive, magical.

Awakening the dream image with active imagination

In addition to association, I employed the art of *active imagination*. Jung considered active imagination essential for approaching dream images as though they are real and have a life of their own. Active imagination is the process for delving into the imaginal realm, a portal to the source of creative intelligence yearning to be experienced. Active imagination arouses, enthuses, and animates dream images. It invites us to engage the dream image by viewing it like a movie. The more we engage the images, the more we are energized and captivated by their presence.

For example, with snake, I told it I was frightened and asked it *why* it was appearing. Because it was a threatening figure, I knew I had to be patient and persistent and not expect an instant response. My goal was to cultivate a connection with the image, not judge it or distance from it. Again, this is where a curious stance becomes very important. Aizenstat writes, "When we tend to these core images, we open the doors to our true sense of self ... It makes us discover unique ways of responding. We are pushed to access new abilities, find new resources, and expand our boundaries."

Engaging snake in daily life reduced my anxiety and fear. Living close to the Pacific Ocean, I often see large pieces of Pacific kelp lying across the beach. Active imagination inspired me to see these as snake-like representations, and in the bright light of day I felt safe enough to befriend them and include them in dialogue. I did the same thing with the green succulents that draped gracefully in an inverted "U" along my hiking trail. The more I used active imagination, the more I forged an intimate relationship with snake. Further, in my thirst for understanding these myriad snake images, I learned that in some ancient cultures the serpent is seen as the most universal and auspicious archetype, one that symbolizes rebirth and transformation. Snakes shedding their skin represent the power of birth, death, and rebirth. Such transformation occurs when the snake's eyes begin to cloud over, and for many shamans this reveals the ability of snake to traverse the realms of life and death. As natural shape-shifters, snakes are honored for being able to both journey below the earth's surface (aka. the underworld) and bathe in the sunlight of the upper world.

Elevating the dream image to the divine daimon

Each life is formed by its unique image, an image that is the essence of that life and calls it to a destiny. As the force of fate, this image acts as a personal daimon, an accompanying guide who remembers your calling.
—James Hillman

In ancient Greek culture, a *daimon* is replete with wisdom and acts as a facilitator between the earthly and the divine. Daimons possess special knowledge and our dream images contain a stream of energy that at times may be seen as our own personal daimon. When we use association and active imagination we bring our dream images to life; it's akin to taking the hand of a shadow on the wall and inviting it to step away from the wall and walk with us awhile. As it walks beside us, we can dialogue with it and probe the deeper meaning of its presence, and in doing so, it has the potential to become our daimon as we journey toward wholeness.

Through the process of association and active imagination, snake has become a daimon for me. It has shifted from a nightmarish figure to one that points the way forward when I am out of balance emotionally, mentally, physically, or spiritually and it hasn't happened easily or quickly. During my snake-dream journey, I found a picture of an albino python (considered harmless) wrapped around the shoulders of a lovely woman. I printed the picture and framed it, a tribute to the first snake dream I had in August, 2013. Today, it still sits proudly on my fireplace reminding me of the transformation that can occur from tending to our dream images. Dream work requires practice, patience, and curiosity and is worth every drop of effort you are willing to expend. Your dream images possess intelligence and insight which can illuminate every area of your life. Connecting to them will energize you and provide information that expands your entire human experience.

Put it into practice!

Think about a positive dream image.

- What feelings emerge when you think about this image?
- Tap into your body and notice if you can feel the image. Pay attention to your feet, stomach, and chest.
- Let the image know you are curious and invite it to share its wisdom by asking, "Who is visiting now?" "What is happening here and why are you appearing now?"
- What action can you take on behalf of the image?
- Continue working with this image via association and active imagination until you receive the message(s) it desires to share.

Once you are comfortable engaging non-threatening dream images you can begin working with confusing, disturbing, or alarming ones. Frightening images have the greatest charge and are crucial not to ignore or diminish because they provide invaluable insight and they won't go away! The form of the image may shift, but the underlying fear they trigger will not. (See more on nightmares in Chapter 7.)

Dream images can be metaphorical, mythical, and archetypal—they arrive, surprise, and keep us feeling alive. Your dream images plummet through defenses, revealing all, excluding nothing. These phantasmagorias reflect our human imperfections, sometimes haunting us and chafing at the fragile strands of our ego. Most importantly, these nightly impressions are nocturnal imaginings that possess the power to entertain and enliven, teach and empower, heal and restore.

CHAPTER SEVEN

Nightmares: supportive screams from the unconscious

You learned to run from what you feel, and that's why you have nightmares. To deny is to invite madness. To accept is to control.

—Megan Chance

Nightmares occur when intense energy bangs up against psyche's door. Appearing during (and before) times of transition, nightmares occur more frequently than most of us are aware. Not only do they surface when we feel wracked with fear, but also when we are upset, anxious, feeling confused or overwhelmed. Nightmares do not happen overnight; we have countless dreams warning us about a physical illness, financial failure, or relationship breakdown before the unforgettable nightmare emerges. The problem is, we resist remembering or working with our dreams.

Nightmares are repeated messages from the unconscious, and at times they literally "scream" at us (or make us want to scream) when we turn a deaf ear to the signals in our waking day or nighttime dream life. Not surprisingly, the more we're willing to recall and understand our dreams, the less likely we'll experience them. Nightmares have a unique way of triggering an emotional response; our body reacts with a quickening pulse, sweaty palms and feet, and elevated blood pressure.

71

All of this stems from the fear and adrenaline moving through our physical, mental, and emotional energy centers.

Research reveals that 50% of your dreams can be classified as nightmares. In reality, this depends on the individual. Dreams are sometimes broadly classified as nightmares whenever the dreamer is afraid. Certain personalities appear to be more prone to nightmares than others, for example, people who are highly sensitive. From my own experience with dream analysis, this may simply be true because these individuals are more apt to recall their dreams. I have noticed people who are less sensitive to their thoughts and feelings sometimes have more difficulty recalling their dreams, so it is possible that they're having nightmares but not remembering them. Also, stress, PTSD, and trauma play a major factor in the occurrence of nightmares in both children and adults.

Children have more nightmares than adults. The occurrence is high in childhood and often declines as children age. Internationally known researcher on dreams, Dr. Ernest Hartmann, states that nightmares are particularly evident between the ages of three to six. Monsters lurking in the dark, scary shadow figures hiding under the bed, and being chased or hurt by large creatures seem to be common nightmare themes. Considering the uncertainty and fear that children are prone to makes them vulnerable.

Nightmarish themes

Nightmares stem from persistent inner conflict within the dreamer. Fear of confrontation, feeling controlled or manipulated by another, feelings of powerlessness, or an imbalance within psyche can cause nightmares. Below is a list of common nightmare themes that discuss some of these fears.

- Being pursued or chased by a shadow figure, person, or animal
- Feeling trapped or suffocated
- Falling, drowning, or burning to death
- Being attacked by a person, animal, or monster, witch, beast
- Car accidents
- War, genocide
- Environmental disasters, for example, tornado, tsunami, hurricane, earthquake
- Public humiliation.

This is a very short list of possible nightmare themes and as I mentioned, every dream story and image is personal to the dreamer. So your partner who loves skydiving may not find free-falling 30,000 feet during his dream to be fear-provoking, as you might. Also, the above list covers themes, not images. And as we discussed in Chapter 6, dream images carry their own personal power and can be frightening for a multitude of reasons.

A client who was an attorney in Santa Barbara and had recently left a law firm to practice on his own had the following nightmare:

> *I am in San Francisco and it's gloomy like a movie scene after a nuclear holocaust. I'm driving a BMW and, taking advantage of the car's power, I zip in and out of traffic. I'm in the left lane of a one-way street and accelerate to pass the cars next to me, moving into the right lane just in time.*
>
> *Now I'm walking on an arched bridge and a man begins to harass me. I tell him I have nothing to give, so he leaves me alone. But now he returns with two other men and they grab me and throw me on a porch that appears to be part of a gift shop. They circle me and push me until I stumble backward, tripping and landing on my back. My legs are up in the air and as one man rushes toward me, I catch him with my feet and with all my might I extend my legs and he goes flying. He flies across the room and takes out the other two men. This is my chance to escape so I run to the door and once outside, I turn right and head down an alley into darkness.*

Unpacking this nightmare which my client referred to as "The Day After" dream, we discussed his thoughts and feelings and discovered in this dream sequence:

Dream Scene 1:

- Landscape is San Francisco = creative, liberal, open-minded, entrepreneurs, expensive
- Holocaust = destroyed environment
- BMW = lifestyle, fast, powerful way of traveling through life, confident
- One way street = limiting thoughts, only one way to travel through life

Dream Scene 2:

- Arched bridge, nighttime = crossing into the shadow realm
- Man = masculine shadow aspect that wants something
- Two more men = increased masculine aspects which feel unsafe, dangerous
- Gift shop = place where some kind of "gift" is being offered
- Lying on back and pushing men off = dreamer feels helpless yet is able to push back.

Delving into the nightmare more deeply, we find that my client was experiencing growth pangs from establishing his own law practice. He was taking on more clients than he could comfortably handle and he disliked saying "No" to his clients. His greatest anxiety stemmed from not having any information to "give" his clients when a deadline was due. The nightmare exposed his desire for wanting a comfortable life-style in which he felt powerful and confident, yet if we break down the word "holocaust" we see that it was "costing" my client "a whole lot." His masculine shadow aspects represented his limiting thought patterns which were pushing him down, inhibiting his ability to set realistic expectations for himself and boundaries with his clients. The "gift" in the nightmare was the dreamer's recognition that even though he felt powerless, he possessed enough inner strength to "push" back. He was able to confront his masculine shadow aspects which had been holding him down and sabotaging his success. However, the nightmare concluded with him walking into a dark alley so he was still not "seeing the light" about the entire situation.

Over the following year, my client had similar dreams involving his masculine shadow sides and as his self-awareness increased, he began to see that he needed to positively integrate them into his work life. Rather than pushing them away in self-defense, he began to see how they could help him take action. He began taking three steps:

1) Coming to terms with the fact that if he wanted to expand, he needed to hire some experienced professionals and pay the price that was required for such talent.
2) Setting realistic boundaries with his clients by not promising to deliver more than he could give in a specific time frame.

3) Having faith and trust that everything would get done and that he could take time to enjoy his life instead of constantly fretting over his workload and performance.

Integrating these three practices (he chose "three" to represent the three shadow aspects in the nightmare) cultivated strength and confidence and within a few months, the nightmares ceased.

Safely facing the fear

Again, one of the worst things you can do is ignore your dreams, but even more destructive is the temptation to blow off your nightmares. They will keep recurring with greater intensity, and if they go unheeded, destructive waking life situations may occur. At the very least, you will continue to be conflicted in some way and blocking an important opportunity for personal development. Ask yourself: "What nightmare am I currently living?" Are you feeling overwhelmed by something or someone, out of control by an addiction, for example, alcohol, food, spending money, sex/porn, work, exercise, drugs/pharmaceuticals, and/or relationship? In working with clients, I have discovered nightmares often surface when the dreamer is feeling powerless in a situation such as by an addiction, or, giving their power away to someone, like an authority figure. More recently, I am finding people who share a deep affinity for nature are experiencing nightmares about the environment, including dreams of overpopulation and death and extinction from massive global warming.

For example, while facilitating a dream group a few years ago, one woman shared the following dream:

> I have replaced all of my lawn with drought resistant foliage to conserve water where I live in California. I've spent a lot of money on this project and decide to walk outside and admire the transformation. But as I walk on to my patio, I see row after row of plants dying from thirst. I realize the drought has not ended and the plants cannot withstand the lack of water. I feel devastated. Then I look up to the hill that sits behind my backyard and see a crowd of people: it's huge and there must be over 1,000 people standing on this small hilly space. They are pointing to something in my yard and I turn to see my hot tub overflowing with hot water! There is water everywhere and I'm trying to figure out how to get the water onto the dying plants.

The dreamer confided she was struggling with an actual drought that was happening in her community along with a nearby open space that was about to be developed into a neighborhood. She had voiced her concerns about the bulldozing of land at some local council meetings, but felt powerless in stopping it from happening. Since she was depressed, we began using her dreams as tools for reconnecting with the environment to defuse her upset as discussed in the following section.

Defusing the dread

Since ignoring our nightmares is unwise, how do we address them in a way that feels safe? Because they are coming from the unconscious (and this can be the individual and/or the collective unconscious), how do we address the fear wrapped around the dream and its images? Think about my client who was deeply disturbed by the figures of the brand new plants dying from thirst while the hot tub was overflowing with water.

Put it into practice!

Take action

Fear has a way of paralyzing us. Anxiety causes us to numb out or shut down which only fuels fear. Taking a step forward defuses the fear. For example, if in waking life you discover a loved one has just been diagnosed with a disease, you could reach out and comfort her, begin researching her illness so you better understand it, journal about your feelings, talk to someone who listens deeply, pray—or all of the above. If you're feeling alarmed from a terrifying nightmare, you could write it down, share it with someone you trust, and using association and active imagination you could tend to the most upsetting dream images as I did with my snake dreams discussed in Chapter 6.

In the case of the dreamer and her drought dream, we began gently addressing her troubling dream images, then between sessions, she began creating what clinical psychologist, Mary Watkins, refers to as "restorative eco-therapeutic practices." This included working with others nearby in creating a community garden, holding an eco-support group once per month in her home, and honoring the grief she was carrying about climate change.

Invite a friendly dream figure to join you

Just as we benefit from the support of a loved one while working through challenges, we need kind and welcoming dream images to help us face our nightmare images. When confronting a scary image or dream, invite a friendly figure from a different dream to join you in your journey. Imagine their presence in front of you before working with the frightening image and let them know you want their guidance and support. For example, when I began working with snake, I invited a wise-woman, crone-like figure who has appeared in other dreams to participate while using active imagination. She was present through-out the entire first year I faced the snake. Her appearance provided the strength and courage I needed to encounter this alarming image and I still call on her when dealing with other disturbing dream images.

Hit the "pause" button

As I discussed in Chapter 6, active imagination is a very effective and powerful process for tending to dream images. However, because it is so potent, it can activate fear that might feel overwhelming. For exam-ple, when I first began researching snakes and looking for photos to use during the active imagination process, I started feeling repulsed and panicky. The pictures brought to life the snake dream images so I began hitting the "pause" button by telling the snake image that I was done for now but would return when I was ready. Using pause allowed me to stay in my power center and remain grounded. The key is not to run from the nightmare image, but to let it know that you are strong and willing to face it, *on your terms*. Taking a hiatus, going for a walk, watching a comedy, or doing something that gives you joy are healthy ways to remain centered. Then, when you're ready, you can return to connecting with the image.

Work with an experienced dream counselor

Some of my biggest breakthroughs with nightmares have happened while working with someone who understands the mystical, magical, multifarious realm of dreams. There are many Jungian therapists and dream practitioners who have studied association, active imagination, amplification, and other concrete dream processes that will provide great benefit. (Ideally, they use their own dreams as a tool for growth and transformation.) I do not recommend sending your dreams for analysis to online organizations that "specialize" in dreams. Getting to know you and your life is essential and can only be done working with someone one-on-one or in a small group. Also, you may want to work with a close friend or loved one who does dream work. Because my husband and I are so close we are able to support each other's dream process in amazing ways, unlike someone who does not know me or the issues I am addressing. Finally, consider joining an ongoing dream group. There are countless dream circles which can provide the sustenance needed to support you in your dream process.

Keep in mind that there is much to be gained by exploring your nightmares. They do not occur to hurt you, but to *support* you. Every nightmare contains a gift, a priceless message. Notice them, record them, learn from them, and in doing so you will integrate precious parts of yourself that have been hiding in the wings, waiting to be acknowledged and accepted all along.

CHAPTER EIGHT

Dreams of healing

Addiction: the soul's request for recognition

> *An addiction is anything we do to avoid hearing the messages that body and soul are trying to send us.*
>
> —Marion Woodman

"Laura, the more hardships you can endure the stronger you will become," my maternal grandmother, Virginia Grace, advised me when I was eight years old. Every summer as a child, I would spend two weeks with Grandma Grace in her tiny house in Michigan, across the street from the most yummy candy store I had ever seen. A spindly apple tree grew in her backyard and I would climb it feeling safe and happy, away from my very unhappy home where my parents frequently fought. My mother struggled with unresolved childhood trauma which led to a variety of addictions. I painfully witnessed her artistic and gregarious spirit descend into depression then wither and die at the age of fifty-seven.

Dr. Gabor Maté, a distinguished leader in the addiction field, is a proponent for a compassionate approach toward addiction, whether in ourselves or in others. He works with the most intense inner-city drug addicts in Vancouver and believes addiction is not found in genes, but has its origins in emotional setbacks. "A hurt is at the center of all addictive behaviors," Maté states. "It is present in the gambler, the Internet addict, the compulsive shopper and the workaholic. The wound may not be as deep and the ache not as excruciating, and it may even be entirely hidden—but it's there." Myriad forms of addiction pervade our culture: food, alcohol, sex, work, exercise, shopping, video games, gambling, relationships, perfection ... the list goes on and on. I've even worked with clients who have become addicted to their meditation and yoga practices. Addiction is addiction, regardless of the form, and the need to replace our discomfort (emotional and/or physical) with some form of pleasure drives the desire.

Grandma Grace's sage advice was right; my early childhood challenges were preparing me for a resilient adulthood. By the time I reached thirty, I had survived a variety of painful experiences including my mother's death and a divorce. Some of my coping mechanisms were addictive in nature, and though I never participated in a 12-Step recovery program, I dedicated myself to the recovery of my soul. Dream work became a daily practice and the wisdom flowing through my dream's themes, landscapes, images, and feelings provided remarkable inspiration and guidance.

Dreams of addiction often rear their head when we least expect it. They can be an integral part of the recovery process. Research reveals that addiction dreams emerge even when a person appears to be doing well in a recovery program. Yet, because the unconscious speaks to us through our dreams, drinking, drugging, or gambling in dreams can help us see that we may be heading toward a ditch on the road to recovery.

Dreaming of addictive behaviors can also illuminate an addiction we're not even aware we have. For example, a client named "Allison" was concerned about her alcohol consumption. She considered herself a social drinker who enjoyed great food and fine wine with good friends. A hard worker and responsible mother, Allison functioned at a high level and wasn't concerned about being addicted until she was in her early forties. When she came to see me, we began exploring her daily stressors and nighttime dreams. Over a four-month period she had a series of dreams about her drinking:

> I'm with my family and we're on vacation in northern California. Wanting to be present and enjoy my time with them, I decide not to drink much wine during our trip. My son is acting rebellious and trying to control what I say and every time I begin to speak, he shushes me. My husband is

drinking beer and having a good time. I'm upset because we agreed that
neither of us would have very much alcohol on this vacation. The more he
drinks, the louder he becomes and I feel let down. Yet my teenage kids think
he's a lot of fun and I look like a wet blanket. I want to escape but know that
my family will be mad at me for leaving. I feel trapped.

Allison's dreams helped her face her dependence on alcohol, a painful revelation. She began to question whether or not she was an "HFA," a popular term in our society for a high functioning alcoholic. Because her dreams were often about her husband's abuse of alcohol, it would have been easy for Allison to deny having a problem. Yet she recognized in waking life her husband consumed very little alcohol. As we gently probed her dreams, Allison recognized that her "inner husband/male" was representing a vital aspect of herself. She connected the dots between her desires for wine at the end of the day as a reward for working hard. Not surprisingly, her animus—the doing/productive/busy part of her—was becoming intoxicated in her dreams. Together, we began addressing three important areas: Allison's workload, the time she spent taking care of others, and an old childhood wound.

Tending to psyche, soma, and soul with dream images

Allison felt disconnected from her soul and was hungry for something truly nourishing. Allowing her dream images to guide her, she began listening to the "big dream images" that spoke to her. Marion Woodman suggests dream images are alive within the body of the dreamer, and recovering the energy contained within the image promotes healing: physically, emotionally, and spiritually. These nocturnal metaphors become a transforming vehicle for the dreamer because according to Woodman, dream images live *in* the body. Woodman herself suffered from anorexia and recovered from it by working with her dream images. She once quipped, "I love working with addicts, because I used to be one myself." Her life's work demonstrates how dream images have the capacity to heal both a wounded body and spirit.

Through a series of guided visualizations, Allison began connecting with her dreams somatically, paying particular attention to how specific dream images felt inside her body. She first noticed how the images directed her to the places where she was holding anxiety and tension. Next, Allison tapped into the energy of the image. For example, a dream image she gravitated toward was a cobalt blue triangle which gave her the essence of power and joy. Through guided imagery, Allison envisioned the triangle in different places in her body, mainly her lower abdomen and solar plexus, and the more she worked with the image, the more alive she felt. She painted a cobalt blue triangle onto a canvas and hung it in her home office where she could see it every day. We also harnessed the energy of the triangle as Allison talked about her past and the abuse she experienced as a young child. At the same time, she sought the counsel of a wise therapist who was trained in addictions. Eventually, instead of using alcohol as a reward at the end of the day, Allison began writing music and making jewelry from sea glass she found along the shoreline near her home.

Addiction is complex and exists on myriad levels. Everyone dealing with addiction suffers. I have immense compassion for the pain that accompanies addiction and have witnessed how it can destroy people's lives and the lives of everyone around them. There is no easy solution to healing addiction and I do not claim that working with dreams will heal all addictions. However, *dream work is soul work and all addiction disconnects us from soul*. Addiction is the soul's loudest request for recognition. Our nighttime dreams are the vernacular of the soul and learning to speak its language can call forth a life imbued with purpose, rich with meaning, and return us to our authentic selves.

The abaton

In the end, the examined life—the task Healing Dreams set vividly before us—is ours alone to reject or embrace; which we way choose makes all the difference in the world.

—Marc Ian Barasch

Millennia ago, the ancient physician, Asklepius, performed miraculous healings in the numinous dream incubation container called the *abaton*. Greek for "inaccessible," the abaton was the sacred vessel inside a temple reserved only for priests. And though it was widely used an epoch ago, it still exists today. In the sanctuary of our very own bed, we have the opportunity to receive healing dreams, not just for our physical health, but for recovering our emotional, spiritual, creative, and soulful selves. Experiencing such restoration while dreaming is not far-fetched if we look at the word "clinic." The etymology stems from the Greek word *kline* meaning a "bed" or "couch" where dreams occur.

And whether or not we believe it is the healer Asklepius, the divine physician or our higher self, we know *psyche* bestows us with dreams to help us heal just as it did during ancient Greece.

Psyche is active when the waking ego is sleeping, and all symptoms, whether an aching back or a broken heart, always lead to psyche. In ancient healing, Asklepius tended not only to the body, but to psyche and soul as well. People would incubate for hours or days in a ritual container waiting for a healing dream to occur. The healing dream they waited for was not just an ordinary dream, but a significant dream often involving an archetype. Asklepion physicians were also master dream interpreters. They worked with specific totem animals that visited the patients while they slept including the rooster, dog, and the famous image we see wrapped around Asklepius's staff, the snake. Since snakes embody the shedding of something old in order for something new to emerge, it wasn't uncommon for the healing dreams or visions to reveal a snake. This powerful image could lead to a patient's transformation, reconnection to the body and restoration of the soul.

Our inner Asklepius recognizes that our dreams possess the power to repair and renew the fragmented parts within us. They arrive during our slumber whether we invite them or not. They appear, bidding us to remember them before they fade into the realm of never-never land. They reveal their myriad cast of characters ranging from spiritual to sinister. They reappear over and over again, despite the fact that we awake in the morning believing we "didn't have any dreams last night." They enamor, enchant, rouse, delight, frighten, thrill, captivate, enthuse, and confuse. One of my favorite poets, David Whyte, writes, "In that first hardly noticed moment in which you wake, coming back to this life from the other more secret, moveable and frighteningly honest world where everything began, there is a small opening into the new day ... you are not a troubled guest on this earth, you are not an accident amidst other accidents, you were invited from another and greater night than the one from which you have just emerged."

When you awaken tomorrow morning, allow your dreams time to incubate in your private abaton. Lay quietly and feel the dream's energy flowing throughout your body. Be still with the dream without trying to make sense of it, just let it rest silently inside of you. This is how the dream can mend the stressors of life in our manic driven culture, heal the emotional bruises we have experienced along the way, and elevate us into an awakened life.

CHAPTER NINE

Eco-dreams

We do not live in a vacuum nor do we dream in a vacuum. We are interconnected to the web of life. Dreams connect us to the doorway of our ecological self. Because we are often preoccupied with how things are going in our daily lives, dreams can keep us attuned with the natural world. Our human brothers and sisters, animals and the environment appear during dreamtime, reminding us there is a larger awareness in which we are inherently linked. These types of dreams fall into the category of *eco-dreaming* and can shed light upon the current state of our natural environment and the issues of survival we face. Not surprisingly, more and more of my clients are bringing dreams that reveal their concern and anxiety for climate change and the destruction of the natural world.

In *Creating Restorative Ecotherapeutic Practices,* Mary Watkins writes about exploring the effects of "place" on psyche and the psychological suffering that arises from environmental problems. She shares her own journey of personal suffering and how her nighttime dreams were pivotal: "To my surprise and horror I found myself being called by the nuclear peril we have created. Unbidden scenarios of nuclear holocaust bled through my nightly dreams into my daily consciousness. My nightmares were insistent and resistant to being interpreted on only a personal level. As I began to acknowledge my awareness of the vulnerability of our situation and of the horrific nature of our stock-piled weapons, I came to understand psychiatrist and psycho-historian Robert Jay Lifton's concept of 'psychic numbing.'"

Our relationship with the environment sometimes appears most vividly during dreamtime. An example of such dreaming is shown in the following dream:

> *I'm sleeping in my bed when I hear a noise outside my bedroom window. Whoever it is moves from the window to my backdoor and I'm scared they're trying to break in. I can't remember if I locked the door before I went to bed. Next, I hear the door opening and my heart sinks because now I know I forgot to lock the door. It's a very dark night but I don't want the person to know where I am, so I don't turn on the bedroom light. I get out of bed and walk very quietly toward the door and peer into the dark-ness, toward the back door. There is light shining through the window from the starry sky and I see a short, shadowy figure about three feet tall. It looks at me and I can see it is upset.*
>
> *I ask: "Who are you?"*
>
> *It replies: "I live in the dirt."*
>
> *"Where in the dirt?" I inquire, and it responds: "Beneath the tall pine. I live below the shallow roots near the surface."*
>
> *I am perplexed because I know there is a large group of gophers living in the ground and they have been tearing up my yard as never before. I become aware that this is an "earth- woman" who knows me and she is unhappy because I have been ignoring her. She continues communicating, telepathically, telling me I have been so busy with my personal life that I have forgotten about her and the "others" who live below the ground. I turn on a light and she says she has to return to the dark, so I quickly switch the light off and I wake up.*

For the dreamer, the earth-woman represents the deepest, muddiest regions—the landscape of *soul*. James Hillman speaks of the soul and its connection to the moon, the realm of the dead, and dreams of the night. Spirit, he shares, is found in higher education, the corporate ladder, and religious centers. Yet soul is discovered in the murky shadow, the sticky issues of life, and the suffering within our human experience. Earth-woman reflects the dreamer's connection with the natural world. She shared how earth-woman's unhappiness mirrored her own sadness for not spending more time in nature. As much as the dreamer valued nature's positive effects on her mind, body, and spirit, her ultra-busy lifestyle was preventing her from making it a priority. Not surprisingly, she was experiencing more stress and anxiety than usual. This dream was a wake-up call to slow down and immerse herself in the tranquil beauty of the natural world that surrounded her.

Eco-dream work, grief, and resilience

It is not surprising that people who are deeply connected to the natural world are experiencing more frequent dreams about the radical environmental shifts. In my own life, I am dreaming frequently about nature, triggering feelings of profound grief. Wanting to explore this phenomenon, I created a small dream group of four people to explore their dreams and observe images, themes, and feelings pertaining to the environment. Over a three-month period, we met in a beautiful park in Central Coast, California to share our eco-dreaming experiences. Several of the dreams contained both vivid images and feelings as reflected in this dream:

> I am walking outside near my home in a beautiful area, but the terrain is more green and grassy. Other people are around and we are talking, then we look around us and see a very lovely area with homes and realize how expensive it is. Donald Trump is nearby and I am aware of his wealth and how the beautiful land around me is about to be developed. I feel both angry and sad and begin to weep.

The dreamer's psyche was communicating emotions that were distinct and palpable upon waking. She saw the dream as a pathway toward building resiliency during this time of environmental tragedy. She sensed her willingness to grieve would cultivate inner strength, a core aspect of resilience.

Dreams are exposés of our path toward individuation by bringing in the perspective of the unconscious, particularly those which appear as *big dreams*. Jung stated such dreams "prove to be the richest jewel in the treasure-house of psychic experience." Big dreams refer to the psychological conflicts and intense emotions not yet identified or processed by the dreamer. Hartmann reveals that a powerful central image (CI) distinguishes big dreams as being significant in a way which allows us to chart the "bigness" of our dreams. He also delineates these uniquely unforgettable dreams from less significant dreams by breaking them down into four subcategories: *memorable dreams*, defined as dreams remembered for a long time; *important dreams*, defined simply as dreams labeled "important" by the dreamer; *significant dreams*, again as defined by the dreamer; and *impactful dreams*, which are those judged as having a definite impact on the dreamer and his life or work.

Dreams are an integral pathway for integrating psyche, soma, soul, and spirit. In his autobiography *Memories, Dreams, Reflections,* Jung inquires, "Whence comes such a dream?" revealing how dreams bring fresh awareness and insight into his questions and problems. He considers, "Something must therefore have been at work behind the scenes, some intelligence, at any rate something more intelligent than myself." When working with eco-dreams, it's imperative to remain open to dream images which speak to our struggle over environmental destruction. Jung illuminates how "psyche is transformed" from the unconscious through dreamtime. Such dreams inform the dreamer of the need to engage in grief work. Employing the power of metaphor, we can use our eco-dreams to become aware of the subtle voice of the unconscious, beckoning ourselves to feel our feelings—*all of them*—from the fulfillment of standing amidst a tranquil forest of pine trees, to the anger and grief from witnessing the clear cutting of trees. James Hillman (1996) re-visions how we perceive adversity, and suggests that perhaps our challenges are preparing us for what our soul was born to do. For example, he inquires: "The man married his mother [so to speak], but what if he chose his mother to prepare him to be married to that woman?" Reconfiguring the logic, he reveals an entirely different lens through which to see life's perceived obstacles. Taking his wisdom to heart, we can re-vision the environmental challenges around us. Instead of succumbing to pain and resistance, we can seek to expand our perception, to view the natural world as it is *in this moment*, and appreciate whatever glimmers of beauty we can find. Sharing this practice with my eco-dreamers, I have discovered that grief will continue to emerge during dreamtime, but it is not in vain. It truly is a gift that can helps us develop resilience. The following eco-dream is an example of this phenomenon:

> *I have been hiking along the shoreline and return to my house when I see*
> *a man from the cable company on a pole behind our home. He seems to be*

working on our internet connection. My two cats (whom I no longer have in waking life) seem restless and upset, so I look closer and notice all of the beautiful trumpet flowers growing on a line near the pole. They have been growing strong for the past six or seven years and are really stunning. As the cats become more agitated, I look down toward the ground and see the huge pile of trumpet flowers lying there. The cable man had cut them from the wire they had been growing on! I ask him if he plans on putting them back up, but he ignores me and acts like he doesn't have time for me. I ask, more loudly, if he is going to put the flowers back up and he replies, "I hope not." I look at the ground again and to my horror, the trumpet flowers are still lying on the ground and since he had cut them at their roots, I know they are going to die. I sit down on the floor and begin grieving, and as I do so, my two felines come toward me and curl up on either side of me. I feel their love and realize how beautiful they are and know they have been sent to comfort me.

This dream hints at the initial shift from the tension of the conscious mind remaining stuck in pain, toward psyche's wish to explore unknown aspects of oneself, such as the ability to experience deep gratitude and love amidst adversity. Jung identified one's capacity to sustain such tension and how it can propel new insights about oneself. Using our eco-dreams as a form of self-inquiry, we might ask ourselves: *Is it possible to experience profound appreciation for nature while witnessing environmental destruction? How might I feel gratitude for the wondrous pine tree in front of me as I clearly see it is dying from drought? Is there an entirely new way in which to view environmental destruction through the lens of love and thankfulness?*

Grief for the natural world arises from the awareness of our coexistence with every living thing. Grieving our own sadness for Earth's pain is an essential aspect of resilience. One eco-dreamer wisely commented: "Resilience means constantly reassessing my own inner resilience during these times of great loss and to really look at my own capacities." This aligns with the teaching of deep ecologist Joanna Macy who states: "Planetary anguish lifts us onto another systemic level that opens us to collective experience … Don't apologize if you cry for the burning of the Amazon or Appalachian Mountains stripped for coal. The sorrow, grief, and rage you feel are a measure of your humanity and your evolutionary maturity. As your heart breaks open, you create room for the world to heal."

CHAPTER TEN

The power of somatic dreams

Body-based dream images leave the dreamer with profound somatic sensations that can be absolutely terrifying or highly pleasurable. What may start out as a seemingly simple dream can lead to profound personal insights when the feelings and physical reactions to the dream are worked with somatically.

—Jeanne Schul, PhD.

How often do you have a dream that is so vivid, you can actually "feel" it in your body? Or, when was the last time you awoke and the intensity of the dream left you feeling heavy or encumbered and you were unable to shake it off? We might refer to dreams of this nature as "somatic dreams" since you can literally feel a dream image or occurrence in your body. The snake dream I described in Chapter 1 where I felt the snake's fangs penetrating my left hand is a somatic dream; I continued to "feel" the bite for weeks after I dreamt about it. These are incredibly powerful dreams and can lead to transformation when properly understood because the *body becomes the point of contact with the unconscious*. Somatic dream work entails remembering the body and recalling its voice. Our somatic dreams offer us guidance along the path of becoming more fully who we are capable of being. They create unforgettable sensations within the dreamer's body. The following dream is an example:

> It is nighttime and I am walking outside. The streets are hilly, like San Francisco, and my partner and daughter are ahead of me when I spot a female lion. She is quite large and I am startled to see a lion in a residential section. She looks right at me and I am afraid and trying to discern if she is going to attack me. I desperately hope she is not hungry.
>
> We gaze at each other, eye-to-eye, and I begin telling her not to be afraid. She gives me a long look and begins slowly walking toward me and I realize she is hungry. "Oh god, oh no," I think to myself.
>
> I see my partner at the bottom of the hilly street and begin calling for him. As I yell for him, I can see he is looking up and moving toward me, but doesn't see the lion. She is coming closer and gets on top of me. She is incredibly strong and I know I am about to be eaten. My partner now sees her and is walking toward me, but she already has her mouth on me. I feel her teeth sinking into my upper thigh and then into my abdomen. As her teeth sink into my flesh I realize I am going to die by being eaten alive by this lion.
>
> I say out loud to God, "Okay, I need to surrender," but I keep resisting.
>
> I yell for my partner but he cannot save me. I am moaning from the pain of her teeth mauling me, and as the dream ends I notice the lion's eyes are yellow and very close together. She is staring at me with fierce intensity, I am mesmerized by her eyes. As I begin to wake up, I am moaning out loud from the pain as she mauls me. My thighs and abdomen ache as I awaken from the dream.

Since somatic dreams shine a light on physical symptoms and psychological issues which are unconscious, I engaged the dreamer in a process I call *dream inquiry:*

> What is the core essence or energy of this image? What is its emotion or mood? What am I feeling while focusing on the image? How might I describe the particularity of this image? Using my senses, what am I smelling, hearing, and seeing while focusing on the lion mauling my upper thigh and abdomen? What are the distinct attributes of the lion, that is, size, weight, color, shape, markings, and texture? What is the lion trying to convey? What might the lion have to do with my life right now? What insights arise as I observe the image?

Second, we "moved" the dream image which enabled the dreamer to engage the psyche-soma connection. Again, this allows the body to be the contact point with the unconscious. As the image moves through the dreamer's psyche and soma, it carries energy that can support the dreamer's psychological development. The dreamer moves the image while remaining intently open and aware to messages and meaning being communicated.

The findings from this dream revealed the need to more deeply surrender to the dreamer's "animal," or, inner instincts. The more she began trusting her gut (abdomen), the more she could move forward (thighs). As previously mentioned in Chapter 3 in "spiritual dreams," the color yellow is associated with a sense of self and personal power. It also aligns with the quality "I CAN."

For the dreamer, "lion" symbolized courage and was expressing her inner "hunger" for trusting her intuition and inner strength to carry her forward during a challenging time in her life.

In the next section, we examine how moving the dream image can lead to transformation.

Awakening by "moving" the dream image

Nighttime dreams provide raw, organic, soul-energy and when worked with somatically, they open a gateway to higher levels of consciousness. For example, something I teach my clients during dream sessions and retreats entails a process called embodied dream movement. Focusing on a specific dream image, participants are taught how to "move" an image. Doing so deepens the psyche-soma connection because the dreamer engages a dream image as though it is alive *in the body*.

You don't need to be a seasoned dreamer to work somatically with your dreams. I will illustrate the process in the following example. One of my clients shared a vivid dream scene where he was riding in a large powerboat being driven by his father. As they approached the lighthouse, he saw a whale breach. Although this dream image sounds pleasant, we discussed what he was feeling during his waking life. He shared that he felt trapped: His desire was to shift from working long hours at a law firm to becoming a chef. Since childhood, his passion was cooking and baking which he only had time to enjoy on the weekends. Time was ticking away and he feared he would be stuck in a high-paying job that left him feeling low. In addition, his financial responsibilities were significant; his mortgage payment was several thousand dollars per month and he was paying for his daughter to attend an expensive college on the East Coast.

Using the embodied dream process, I stood up and asked the man to get up on his feet. I then encouraged him to lean into his experience of feeling trapped and to tell me if he felt any sensation in his body. He stated he felt constricted around his neck and shoulders and that he had been struggling with shoulder pain the past couple of months. I then invited him to close his eyes and move in whatever way he wanted while feeling the tightness in his upper body. He crouched down and I mirrored his movement by crouching down with him. While he was in a crouched position, he wrapped his arms around his body and I asked him what he was feeling physically. He said he felt like a very dense physical ball, tight, confined, and powerless and that his back was aching. I asked him what he was feeling emotionally and he replied, "Sad." I inquired, "What age are you?" And he responded, "I am about eighteen years old. My dad wants me to pursue a career in business like he did."

As the embodied dream process unfolded, we gradually moved from a ball of sadness into a standing position on more solid ground. I invited my client to recall the whale breaching and to move his body so it captured his experience. Together, we raised our arms straight up over our heads and jumped. The image of the magnificent mammal breaching inspired both of us and I invited him to repeat the movement while noticing any sensations in his body. The tightness in his shoulders began to dissipate and he shared that he felt a spark of hope about his future. Like the breaching whale, he could rise up from the depths of the sea and change the course of his destiny; he need not remain shackled by the path he had blazed decades ago, there was still time to navigate a new course of direction. It wouldn't be easy and it wouldn't happen quickly, but working with his dreams provided the light that would guide him toward a safe harbor where his soul resided.

Put it into practice!

- Pick a dream image that calls to you.
- Pay particular attention to what you are feeling, emotionally and physically, when you think about this image.
- What sensations do you feel in your body?

- Using your body as an instrument and the dream image that calls to you as your guide, allow yourself to gently move. It might be uncomfortable and you may feel silly, but keep going. The dream image has a life-force of its own and by mimicking it, your body will move in accordance with its energy. You can perform this exercise alone or with a partner. The partner plays the role of witness and carefully observes your movement. When you are finished moving, the witness describes what she or he experienced during your movement. Quite often, brand new insights arise within the witness who views the dream image from an entirely personal and unique standpoint.

- Dream images often symbolize repressed desires which yearn to become conscious. Since they are created out of pure energy, it's important to go where the energy is and *moving* the image hones directly into their energy. In their book *Dreams, a Portal to the Source,* dream experts Whitmont and Perera remind us that energy flowing into dream images can provide specific messages of various kinds which assist the dreamer with "problem solving, artistic inspiration, psychological development and spiritual deepening."

Treating physical pain with Somatic Dream Expression™

Potently insightful, dreams not only uncover health issues, they point the way to healing. "Once we get used to listening to our dreams," Marion Woodman states, "our whole body responds like a musical instrument." I have witnessed clients heal physical discomfort using dream images and somatic movement. Employing the image as a tool for awareness, they recover blocked energy which opens the doorway for healing. Over the years, this insight inspired me to create a process called Somatic Dream Expression™. An intuitive process, Somatic Dream Expression™ employs dream metaphors, guided imagery, and physical movement, and has proven to be an effective vehicle for addressing physical pain.

For example, a client came to see me while experiencing pain in his right arm. He had recently begun working with his dreams, and after our third session he had a significant dream he recalled in vivid detail:

> I am on a golf course with an older couple and my ex-wife. The older couple tees off first and then my ex tees off and hits the ball shorter than usual. "Blooper" I think to myself, "she typically hits it better than that."

While my ex is still at the tee, I'm feeling impatient and get ready to tee off. She says, "Whoa, wait a second," and I respond, "I'll wait." Truthfully, I'm in a hurry so I move toward the tee before my ex walks off. I quickly hit the ball and whiff it, and feeling embarrassed, I want to hit it again. The older man says, "You whiffed it." I respond, "Yes, count one." Then, I barely line up to take another swing before I hit the ball again—Whack— and it slices to the right. I'm feeling frustrated, constricted, and defeated, and then I wake up.

Using free association we focused on the key dream images and recorded his thoughts, perceptions, and feelings that surfaced from the most important images:

- Golf course: Pretty, comfort, safety, familiar, past, childhood, comfortable, lack of confidence, wishful past, missing playing golf, regret, professional player, happiness.
- Older couple: Authority, parental figures, judgment, observing, critical, elders.
- Ex-wife: Past, marital mistake, disempowered, blooper, empty, emotional flatness, good golfer.
- Golf swing: Anxious, tight, overly confident, constricted, confused, mystery, disconnect between mind and body, hurry up.
- Whiff: Embarrassment, missing the mark, wasting life, hurts, regret, loss of energy, lethargic, depressing, lack of purpose, "What's it all for?", leaking energy, passionless.

During free association, some defenses arose regarding the older couple and ex-wife. As we talked about his resistance, it became clear the dreamer was still carrying some resentment toward his father. While working for a large automotive company, he hated his job but stuck it out, a behavior he perceived as a victim and martyr. Also, as an executive, his father felt forced to relocate the family on several occasions. One of the relocations occurred when the dreamer was a teenager and active in high school. The relocation caused a significant amount of stress. At the same time, he was frustrated how his parents kept encouraging him to enter the "safe" realm of business versus the "risky" domain of professional golf, a path he followed but always regretted.

Somatic Dream Expression™ emphasizes the healing power from identifying bodily sensations while remaining focused on a dream metaphor. Using guided imagery, the dreamer relived hitting the golf ball then "whiffing" it, while noticing the pain in his arm. After practicing this technique several times, he then envisioned taking the stroke and feeling it in his body while reexperiencing the frustration he felt in his dream from whiffing the ball. Whiffing the ball mirrored the rigidity he felt in his arm, so we began "moving" the dream image of hitting the ball. The dreamer slowly raised his arm as if taking a swing while standing surefootedly on the floor in my office. With each gentle swing, he visualized hitting the ball smoothly while his body gradually shifted from rigidity to fluidity. Focusing on the *metaphor* was an essential part of the process.

Marion Woodman teaches that the inherent healing gift of metaphor and dream images affect us on three levels: mental, emotional, and imaginative. Seeking meaning and interpretation is an essential part of the mental sphere, while the emotional arena enables us to connect with the feelings embodied in the metaphor. Finally, from the power of the imaginal realm we are able to experience transformation and healing. All of this occurs when the body is in movement and acts as a vehicle for psyche. "Metaphor means transformer," Woodman emphasizes. "The image, the metaphor, comes in one way, moves through the transformer, is changed and comes out at another level. This is where healing lies, within ourselves."

After several sessions of Somatic Dream Expression™, the dreamer began to gain some emotional clarity. For him, "whiffing the ball" meant "whiffing life." He had been feeling out of balance with his creative and feminine aspects—the receptive, nurturing, comforting, intuitive parts of himself. He had been working very hard at expanding his business and was feeling burned out, defeated, and was tempted to give up, a pattern he had carried since youth. As a boy, he loved golfing and was offered a golf scholarship, yet his fear caused him to forsake his dream. Fear of failure or fear of success, he wasn't sure, yet either way, some of the same fears were still alive within him including his fear of growing his business. It was also apparent he was carrying some grief as well: sadness from having not pursued his passion and choosing a "safe" career.

Through image-association and Somatic Dream Expression™, the dreamer felt the pain in his body begin to shift and his constricted arm muscles soften. He learned how to scan his body and make some significant physical-emotional connections. The tension and pain began to move from his arm down to his legs. We continued using Somatic Dream Expression™ to ground his body so he felt more balanced and supported. Shifting his attention between swinging the club and feeling his emotional reaction, he continued until his bodily sensations and movements resolved to a point of feeling grounded and stabilized.

Each time, the dreamer was able to move his arm more freely and with less pain. In between our sessions, he journaled about his pent-up sadness regarding the past. Eventually, he replaced his fears of expanding his business with optimism and gratitude, and simultaneously, the physical pain dissipated.

As we develop a relationship with our dreams, we learn how to incorporate them as incredible tools for healing. And like a healthy, loving relationship, dream work requires patience, commitment, and humility. The pain in this dreamer's arm did not happen overnight, it resulted from years of old programming, regrets, perfectionism, and pushing himself too hard. Similarly, healing his pain did not happen immediately. He harnessed the courage to peer beneath the surface and trust in the wisdom of his dreams. Just like this man, the more we engage in a meaningful relationship with our dreams and employ their intelligence with respect, the more psyche blesses us with its healing wisdom.

CHAPTER ELEVEN

Accelerating your awakening through Waking Dreaming™

We can do a lot of practice in our sleep! We are also doing deep practice when we learn to navigate by synchronicity and look at the everyday world around us as a set of dreamlike symbols.

—Robert Moss

Did you know that your nighttime dreams and daytime experiences are completely interconnected? They appear to exist at opposite ends of the continuum which is why we tend to discount or ignore them. But indigenous peoples like the Aboriginal Australians embody *The Dreaming* or *Dreamtime* which describes the web of life between the numinous and natural worlds. In essence, there is no difference between being asleep versus being awake; it's all one big dream. Similarly, shamans believe the dream world and the spirit world are exactly the same and that we are dreaming the world into being. This is why for thousands of years indigenous peoples knew they could count on receiving wisdom from their ancestors, guidance from spiritual realms, and valuable answers to mystifying questions. Solutions can arise from the liminal phase of "hypnagogia" which has its roots in Greek etymology meaning "guide." There are two distinct periods: "hypnagogic" signifying the period of being led into slumber and "hypnopompic" meaning "away from sleep." Both interludes last mere minutes as your mind floats between "waking" and "sleeping."

The "twilight zone"—the hypnopompic zone when we are stirring from our slumber but not fully awake—is an exciting interval. This marvelous cycle opens the portal for experiencing innovative break-throughs and discoveries and is a time when we make connections that escape the ordinary conscious mind. Thomas Edison, Salvador Dali, Albert Einstein, and countless others have found this in-between state to be the perfect space to unearth resolutions to problems and foresee visions about the universe.

However, answers, ideas, and insights are *not* limited to nighttime dreams or the liminal states. A potent practice I created called Wak-ing Dreaming™ leads to heightened wakefulness and enhances your nighttime dream recall and understanding. "Those who have compared our life to a dream were right," Michel de Montaigne once affirmed. "We sleeping wake, and waking sleep." I have used Waking Dreaming™ and taught the process to my students for more than twenty years. It is highly effective and embodies the power of synchronicity. Waking Dreaming™ is aimed to liberate us from the misconception that our waking life experiences are merely random and passive.

Synchronicities: bridging your inner and outer worlds

Pause now to ask yourself the following question: "Am I dreaming or awake, right now?" Be serious, really try to answer the question to the best of your ability, and be ready to justify your answer.

—Stephen LaBerge

The term *synchronicity* was coined by Jung to express the idea of a causal relationship between "two or more psychic and physical phenomena." Jung witnessed the birth of this conception while supporting a patient whose animus (inner male) was rigid and fearful and blocking her from accessing her deeper self. During therapy, she told Jung how she had dreamt of a golden scarab. The very next day, a live scarab hit against Jung's window. He was surprised to see that it was a golden scarab which was unheard of for that particular environment and climate zone. Connecting the patient's scarab dream with the waking experi-ence, he recognized how the scarab symbolized the concept of death and rebirth; the same phenomenon needed for his patient to break free from her rigid ego and belief system in order to delve deeper into her inner self. This seeming coincidence paved the way for what we now recognize as the power of "synchronicity."

While traveling through your daily waking life you possess the capacity to witness experiences from a heightened level of awareness. Most of us are asleep; emotional setbacks and trauma can disconnect us from our deeper selves causing us to sleepwalk through life. Working with your nighttime dreams engages your soul and brings to life what I call "soul spark." Soul sparks inspire new perspectives and directions and lead to significant positive changes. Often when I'm working with dream participants in my programs, I see a student's eyes light up when they begin sharing their dreams. They may have entered the room with a flat look in their eyes, but as soon as they talk about a dream that calls to them their eyes reveal a soul spark that has been buried. This makes perfect sense when you remember that dreams emanate from the unconscious and are the language of the soul.

But as I mentioned, nighttime dreams are not the only pathway to awakening. "Awake" is a term we often hear in Buddhism because *Buddha* stems from the root *budh* which means "awake." Buddhism recognizes that in the dream state, the mental body is more fluid and flexible and a time when the imagination is on fire. This raw creative power is greatest in dreamtime. H. F. Hedge once wrote, "Dreaming is an act of pure imagination, attesting in all men a creative power, which if it were available in waking, would make every man a Dante or Shakespeare." However, your waking life also holds infinite opportunity for seeing beyond what cannot be seen. Here is a personal example of Waking Dreaming™:

A few weeks ago I scheduled a session with a friend who is also a soul-coach to discuss some concerns about starting a new venture. She thoughtfully set up two beach chairs and an umbrella along the Pacific shoreline right in front of the rolling waves. The sun began to lower across the sea as I shared how I wanted to integrate some pivotal transformational experiences into my new project. Two large gulls slowly walked across the sand to where we sat and stood quietly, not asking for food, just silently watching us.

Near the end of our meeting, I took a deep breath and exhaled with gratitude, then spotted a whale directly in front of us spouting water. The connection between my grateful exhale and the stream of warm air being blown from the magnificent mammal's lungs (aka the whale's breath) was not lost on us. My heart-centered friend exclaimed, "Look at this amazing synchronicity, the birds and whale are here for you, cheering you on!" Our soulful sharing and peaceful union created the environment that attracted the birds' and whale's validating presence. My inner world and outer worlds were synthesizing, affirming my desire and ability to anchor the transformed aspects of self into my current project.

We need not look very far or hard to see highly personal messages being communicated to us each and every day, hour, and moment. The natural world is a prime environment for witnessing seemingly coincidental connections between our inner and outer worlds. Yet, it reaches far beyond nature; any environment and circumstance will do—from driving down the highway, to conversing with a neighbor, to listening to a podcast. The billboard on the highway, the words your neighbor speaks, and the lyrics in a song are all channels for hearing your soul speak when you're ready to receive it.

Waking Dreaming™ = accelerated awakening

Once upon a time, I dreamt I was a butterfly, fluttering hither and thither, to all intents and purposes a butterfly. I was conscious only of my happiness as a butterfly, unaware that I was myself. Soon I awakened, and there I was, veritably myself again. Now I do not know whether I was then a man dreaming I was a butterfly, or whether I am now a butterfly, dreaming I am a man.

—Zhuangzi, Chinese philosopher

We are in constant contact with the natural world and that natural world is constantly communicating with us. Waking Dreaming™ is a portal to that communication and can be done anywhere and anytime. Let's discuss how this is accomplished.

First, Waking Dreaming™ can be understood the same as your nighttime dreams; symbols are key and are interpreted the same in both waking and sleeping states. The black cat you saw hunting in the backyard this morning can be understood *exactly* the same as the black cat that appeared in last night's dream. This bears repeating: every *daytime* image and experience holds the equivalent and significant meaning as your *nighttime* images and experiences. This may seem hard to believe when we understand how vividly and effortlessly we are able to maneuver through dreamtime versus our waking life. Which is why the Sufi mystic Ibn Arabi declared, "The only reason God placed sleep in the animate world was so that everyone might witness the Presence of Imagination." But psyche relates to image, both sleeping and waking images, and there is no distinct division between the two.

Second, the more familiar you become with the value of your nighttime images, the more you will understand your waking dream images, and, vice versa. Like a continuum, they are interconnected and nurture each other. Waking Dreaming™ augments your nighttime dream awareness by bringing into the conscious what is unconscious.

For example, Thomas and I begin our day by sharing our nighttime dreams. Through deep listening and authentic sharing, we support each other in understanding how the images, archetypes, and themes are attempting to convey vital messages. And because we have been together for more than twenty-five years and are best friends, we recognize each other's issues, fears, hopes, and desires and can provide invaluable feedback. (This is why I recommend a "dream partner," who is a close friend, trusted confidant, or member of a dream group, when you work with your dreams.)

Also, we both employ Waking Dreaming™ as part of our psycho-spiritual practice. For example, a client of mine journals every morning near the ocean and frequently practices Waking Dreaming™ while being in the natural world. Here is a recent example which beautifully illustrates the power of Waking Dreaming™:

Just before starting to journal this morning I read the following from Wayne Muller's book, How Then, Shall We Live?: Four Simple Questions That Reveal the Beauty and Meaning of Our Lives, *and read from the section how the heart of most spiritual practice is simply this: Remember. Remember:*

> *Who you are.*
> *What is true.*
> *What you love.*
> *What is sacred.*
> *How you wish to live.*
> *That you will die and that this day is a gift.*

This passage moved me so I copied it into my journal. As I read on, the book talked about having a touchstone to help center one into remembering. I contemplated this thought but nothing really resonated. As I drove

home from my journaling session I reflected on what I wrote about: remem-
bering who I am, what is true, and how I wish to live. And then, just as
I was thinking those thoughts an amazing hawk flew right in front of the
windshield. I was never in danger of hitting it but the image was vivid.

Using the Waking Dreaming™ process, I reflected, "If this were a
waking dream what would it mean?" What arose was this: "Take seri-
ously those thoughts. Do not let them go. Keep the image of the hawk to
remember. The hawk became my touchstone of remembrance. The universe
just sent me a perfect touchstone to remember who I am at this point in my
life, what is true for me now, and how I wish to live.

Because my client took the time to notice what was happening in the
natural world, he anchored the hawk's presence in his psyche. That
particular morning he had a busy workday in front of him so he could
easily have dismissed the hawk, but he didn't. The hawk was the universe communicating: "Don't ignore this message! Pay attention. Amid
your busy life, hawk is your soul's metaphor for remembering what
you most value." As Jung stated, "In sleep, fantasy takes the form of
dreams. But in waking life, too, we continue to dream beneath the
threshold of consciousness …"

Notice one situation from your waking life that captures your attention. You can start with something very simple like noticing an interesting bumper sticker on someone's car.

- What is written on the bumper sticker?
- How do you feel when you see the words written on it?
- What associations can you make from the bumper sticker?
- Does it trigger any thoughts, ideas, sensations, memories?

Let's fire up the imagination by expanding this example. Imagine you
are driving to the store and in front of you is a red truck. You come to a
stop sign and notice the red truck has a bumper sticker that reads: "Peace
on Earth." Your eyes focus on the word "peace" and you become aware
that lately, you have been feeling stressed out and anything but peaceful.
Then your attention lands on the bright red color of the truck. If this were
a nighttime dream, the color red might symbolize anger. Also, "truck"
is a vehicle and how we "travel" through life and since trucks can carry
things, they often represent "work" or some kind of "load." You quickly
remember how stressful things have been at work and the amount of

frustration you have felt because of your workload. From this perspective, the waking dream is conveying a need to become more conscious of your stress-induced anger and create balance within your work life.

Perhaps it's time to take a vacation, or maybe the waking dream is encouraging you to delegate some responsibility so you can reduce your hours. The situation could also be providing insight to some old patterns you have been carrying about your relationship with work. Seeing the waking dream through this lens may very well guide you to an authentic place of inner "peace."

To summarize, Waking Dreaming™ is a powerful experience for rousing the soul and awakening the mind and heart. It entails the following method and miraculous benefits:

1) Our daily experiences and nighttime dreams are circular and intersect via symbols, archetypes, images, and themes. One realm does not begin where the other one stops; we are continuously dreaming our life into being.
2) Seeing our daily experiences through the same lens as our nighttime dreams is a simple and highly effective process which accelerates our evolving consciousness.
3) The more we practice Waking Dreaming™, the more we will recall and understand our nighttime dreams. Likewise, taking time to unpack our treasure trove of nighttime dreams enables us to more easily interpret our waking dreams.
4) Synchronicities are at the heart of Waking Dreaming™ because they recognize the causal relationship between "two or more psychic and physical phenomena."
5) Both nighttime dreams and waking day situations are teeming with animated information. Waking dreamers recognize this truth and are apt to experience more self-awareness and aliveness.

Put it into practice!

- Select a situation that has an emotional charge to it, something meaningful that you wish to understand more deeply. It could be something challenging like an illness you are dealing with or something joyful such as a recent encounter with an old friend.
- Can you see a theme emerging from the experience? If you were to give it a title, what might you call it?

- What feelings, thoughts, or insights capture your attention?
- What images grab your attention the most?
- As you recall the situation, do you notice any sensations in your body, and if so, where?
- Is there a pearl of wisdom within the experience, some lesson that your inner self is attempting to convey?
- Is there any action being asked of you?
- If you dreamt this experience while sleeping, what might it mean for you?

Waking Dreaming™ is a vital tool for living more consciously and discovering significant purpose and meaning. As important messages are unbound from the unconscious, what appeared mundane becomes numinous. Waking Dreaming™ is a spiritual practice that speaks to the heart, mind, and soul simultaneously, illuminating how we can become conscious of the inner workings of our lives. Practice Waking Dreaming™ and notice the number of meaningful connections you begin to make between your interior life and the external world.

Dreaming of Pegasus and the transcendent nature

Pegasus, the glorious winged creature symbolizing the immortal soul, is the noble guardian of the spirit as it rises to the stars. An adventurous beast, Pegasus was the servant of the gods. Apollo galloped on Pegasus, bringing up the sun each day. In service to Zeus, Pegasus used his power to call forth thunder and lightning needed for the thunderbolts. This most gallant being was cherished for his virtuous contributions and given a constellation in the autumn sky. As my touchstone for writing this book, it provided vitality and animism, bringing life and soul to the dreams that clients and students so graciously shared with me. And it is on this note of heartfelt gratitude that I wish to impart the final dream, shared with me in 2001 by Thomas who dreamt of Pegasus when he was about to embark on a significant move from Michigan to California:

> I'm on the water feeling like I'm in a sailboat race. My boat is more like a surfboard, flat and orange and pink in color. I'm lying on it and paddling with my hands and realize my "boat" has a mast and sail which I haven't raised. I continue paddling and see a sailboat coming up on my left. "Wow, he's coming fast!" As the boat passes I notice it is using a small outboard motor. Then a deep, large wooden motorboat passes me; he's going faster

than me and I see the name "Pegasus" written in gold lettering. I keep
paddling and think, "When I get to the turn I will put my sails up."
I'm feeling "outgunned" by the faster boats then realize there is no wind
so why bother with the sails? But as I continue paddling I shift, then think,
"At the turn, I'll catch the wind" and remain determined to keep paddling.

In dreamtime, Jung believed the image of Pegasus was profoundly enig-
matic, symbolizing spiritual energy which granted access to the realm
of the gods on Mount Olympus. *Pteros* in Greek means "winged" and
hippos means "horse." Combining these two terms we see that Pegasus
is *pterippus* because of his wings, signifying power and mobility. Horses
contain archetypal energy of stability and passion, yet when we add
wings we see the ability to achieve one's highest ideals. Pegasus can
transcend the physical restrictions of the earthly realm by harnessing his mystical capacity. When he appears in dreams, he reveals our
transcendent nature, and the ability to receive sacred inspiration from
our higher selves so we may ascend the limitations and duality of
human life.

Exploring Thomas's dream we discover the following dream images
divulge some inner conflict:

- Landscape: Body of water representing feelings about a current situation. In alchemy, water means *solutio* representing the dissolution of
  old ego structures and a major life transition.
- Sailboat and wooden boats with motor: Sailboats reflect "freedom"
  to Thomas, skimming the unconscious. The boats with motors mean
  they can travel faster than he can.
- Paddling: Using arms to travel instead of harnessing the available
  power of the sails; not traveling quickly enough.
- Tom's boat/surfboard is colored orange and pink: Courageous
  (orange) in order to move forward, faster; pink representing the feminine aspect and the need to listen to his inner feminine aspect.
- "Pegasus" in gold lettering: A horse with wings that can fly above
  the physical realm. Gold is the reward for reaching the destination.

In order to understand this dream, it will help to understand that it is
intertwined with myriad concerns including a significant relationship
issue between Thomas and me. In November 2001, I was ready to take
a leap of faith and relocate to Central Coast, California. Our daughter

had flown the familial nest and now it was just Thomas and me. Having both been born and raised in the Midwest we frequently shared our passion about moving to a new region that challenged us intellectually, emotionally, creatively, and spiritually. Understandably, Thomas was conflicted about leaving his professional life, family, and friends, and moving to a place where there was no job, no family, and no friends. It's not surprising that he felt he had to "paddle" on a small board to reach the outcome, which was getting on "board" with me and my plans. My nature is that of a change agent. This has caused Thomas to spin into a frenzy on numerous occasions simply because at times we operate from a different place of faith and trust. I'm more willing to jump into the river of change when it comes to vocation and living location, and Thomas exhibits more faith when it pertains to our relationship and working through issues.

However, three months later in February 2002, Thomas had a Waking Dreaming™ experience while driving to work. *Peaceful World* by John Mellencamp happened to be playing on the radio and these lyrics that captured Thomas's soul went: "It's what you do and not what you say, if you're not part of the future then get out of the way."

Later that day, Thomas walked into my office, leaned against the door frame and said, "I've been in the way of what our souls have been wanting. I'm on board, let's go." Three months later, we sold everything we owned but our clothes, some plants, and a few pieces of furniture that held sentimental value. In May 2002, we packed our small remains in a U-Haul and hit the road for San Luis Obispo, California. Thirty-five minutes into the journey, hailstones of sleet began cracking against the windshield: we smiled at each other and knew we were on the right path.

Dreams retain infinite wisdom long after we've dreamt them. Thomas's dream is sixteen years old yet still provides profound insight into the path his soul has chosen to take. When he dreamt it, we had no idea of the multifaceted, spiritual meaning of Pegasus, at least, not consciously. Yet, dream images transcend what we have learned, or think we know, because they contain ancient archetypal wisdom. Thomas's dream carries as much significance now, perhaps more, than it did in 2001. It affirms the risk he courageously took at the time along with the depth of connection and commitment we experienced in our marriage. Write down your dreams and save them, they will continue to be a treasure trove of knowledge for the rest of your life.

"Dream" means "music," "joy," and "ghosts." Our dreams allow us to make music out of the visible and invisible realms; they enable us to bring our sacred ghosts or lost parts of ourselves into our awareness so we can integrate all aspects of ourselves into wholeness. Our soul experiences deep fulfillment embarking on a journey without knowing the destination. As Jung proclaimed, "The dream is the small hidden door in the deepest and most intimate sanctum of the soul, which opens to that primeval cosmic night that was soul long before there was conscious ego and will be soul far beyond what a conscious ego could ever reach." May your journey into the realm of dreams be rich in experience, shed light upon darkness, reveal the unknown, and provide soulful fulfillment as you awaken.

Dream template

I. Dream association and self-inquiry

a. Record your dream as if you are recalling a movie clip, using the present tense.
b. Reread your dream description paying close attention to the land-scape, images, characters, colors, words, and feelings. Which aspects "call" to you? Circle them.
c. Underline the *feelings* that arise from your dream.
d. Looking at the *dream images*, which one most captures your attention and what might this image have to do with your life right now?
e. What insights arise as you observe the image?

II. Uncovering the dream's message

a. What is the main *theme* of your dream? (e.g., getting off track with your work/need to find balance, fears about not having enough money, anger is running your life, conflicted about your intimate relationship and afraid of being alone, etc.).
b. What is the most significant *message* this dream is telling you?

c. Reread what you circled and, focusing on your dream theme, write down a possible interpretation.

d. Form an overall conclusion and write down the personal message the dream is offering you.

III. Creating a plan of action

How can you use the main dream image for greater understanding, for example, amplifying the image, active imagination, etc.?

a. Using the personal message, determine the central issue and overall conclusion.

b. Create a plan of action for addressing the central issue.

c. Give thanks for the wisdom and insight your dream is revealing to you.

REFERENCES

Aizenstat, S. (2011). *Dream Tending*. New Orleans, LA: Spring Journal.

Barasch, M. (2000). *Healing Dreams*. New York: Riverhead.

Baring, A. (n.d.). Seminar 10: Rebalancing the Masculine and the Feminine. http://annebaring.com/anbar08_seminar10.htm (retrieved July 8, 2017).

Bosnak, R. (1998). *A Little Course in Dreams*. Boston, MA: Shambhala.

Dass, R. (2014). *Dealing with Fear*. Los Angeles, CA: Love Serve Remember Foundation.

Edinger, E. (1994). *Anatomy of the Psyche*. Peru, IL: Open Court.

Hartmann, E. (2008). The central image makes "big" dreams big: The central image as the emotional heart of the dream. *Dreaming, 18*(1): 44–57. Retrieved from http://search.ebscohost.com.

Hartmann, E. (2008). The Tidal Wave Dream. http://emerald.tufts.edu/alumni/magazine/winter2008/features/dream.html.

Hedge, H. F. (n.d.). http://.quotegarden.com/dreams.html (retrieved September 17, 2017).

Hillman, J. (1979). *The Dream and the Underworld*. New York: HarperPerennial.

Hillman, J. (1989). *A Blue Fire: Selected Writings by James Hillman*. T. Moore (Ed.). New York: Harper & Row.

Hillman, J. (1997). *Dream Animals*. San Francisco, CA: Chronicle Books.

Hyde, L. V. (currently Grace, L. V.) (1997). *Gifts of the Soul*. Grand Rapids, MI: Sustainable Solutions.

Hyde, L. V. (currently Grace, L. V.) (2001). *The Intimate Soul*. Grand Rapids, MI: Sustainable Solutions.

Johnson, R. (1986). *Inner Work*. New York: Harper Collins.

Jung, C. G. (1963). *Memories, Dreams, Reflections*. A. Jaffee (Ed.). New York: Vintage.

Lippman, P. (2000). *Nocturnes: On Listening to Dreams* [e.g., that of Montaine et al. (1700)]. Hillsdale, NJ: Analytic Press.

Macy, J. (2009). Psychotherapy as if the world mattered. In: L. Buzzell & C. Chalquist (Eds.), *The Greening of the Self*. San Francisco, CA: Sierra Club.

Maté, G. (2010). *In The Realm of Hungry Ghosts: Close Encounters with Addiction*. Berkeley, CA: North Atlantic.

Mellencamp, J. (2001). *Cuttin' Heads*. New York: Columbia Records.

Moss, R. (2010). *The Secret History of Dreaming* [e.g., that of Ibn Arabi et al.]. Novato, CA: New World Library.

Namka, L. (2005). *The Mad Family Gets Their Mads Out: Fifty Things Your Family Can Say and Do to Express Anger Constructively*. Tuscon, AZ: Talk Trust and Feel Therapeutics.

Orloff, J. (2011). *Emotional Freedom: Liberate Yourself from Negative Emotions and Transform Your Life*. New York: Three Rivers.

Sartre, J. (1958). *No Exit and Three Other Plays*. New York: Vintage.

Schul, J. (2015). Embodied dreams. In: S. Fraleigh (Ed.), *Moving Consciously: Somatic Transformation through Dance, Yoga and Touch*. Chicago, IL: University of Illinois Press.

Watkins, M. (2009). Creating restorative ecotherapeutic practices. In: L. Buzzell & C. Chalquist (Eds.), *Ecotherapy: Healing with Nature in Mind*. San Francisco, CA: Sierra Club.

Whitmont, E. C., & Perera, S. B. (1989). *Dreams, As a Portal to the Source*. London: Routledge.

Woodman, M. (1988). *The Pregnant Virgin: A Process of Psychological Transformation*. Toronto, Canada: Inner City.

Woodman, M. (1990). *The Ravaged Bridegroom: Masculinity in Women*. Toronto, Canada: Inner City.

Woodman, M., & Dickson, E. (1997). *Dancing in the Flames: The Dark Goddess in the Transformation of Consciousness*. Boston, MA: Shambhala.

Woodman, M., & Sharp, D. (1993). *Conscious Femininity: Interviews with Marion Woodman*. Toronto, Canada: Inner City.

INDEX